VEGANIFICATION®

A Cookbook Celebrating Becoming & Being Vegan

by Linda Voorhis

© 2020 Linda Voorhis, Culinary Instructor & Master Vegan Lifestyle Coach/Educator
All Rights Reserved

ISBN 978-0-578-78791-6

This book or any portion thereof may not be reproduced or used in any manor whatsoever without the express written permissions of the publisher except for the use of brief quotations in a book review.

All recipes created by Linda Voorhis

Designed by Myss Miranda

First Edition, 2020

Published by

Ahimsa Wellness, LLC | Cornville, AZ

VEGANIFICATION.COM

Printed in the United States

This book is dedicated to my hero, my wind beneath my wings, my father, Edward Voorhis. This book would have never come to fruition without his constant unconditional love, support, and encouragement. Although an omnivore, Dad was always up to being my honest taste-tester during my recipe creations and tweaking. Your spirit lives on in these pages.

EDWARD T. VOORHIS, SR.

Born **APRIL 10, 1932**

Earned His Wings **AUGUST 25, 2020**

VEGAN
For the Animals, Planet, Personal Health & Wellbeing

WHILE I DON'T SAY IT FOR THE INGREDIENTS IN THE RECIPES, THIS IS DEFINITELY A VEGAN, 100% PLANT-BASED COOKBOOK

It would be much too cumbersome to continually have the word 'vegan' in front of every ingredient listed in the recipes. It is, therefore, implied that every ingredient used to create these recipes was plant-based with the expectation that they will be recreated by you with the same intention to ensure that no sentient beings are harmed as a result of any of these recipes.

In the Spirit of Ahimsa,

Linda

GREETINGS. My name is Linda Voorhis. I am thrilled to be sharing my two greatest passions with you -- cooking and veganism. From my earliest recollections, I have had a love for cooking. My favorite things to read have always been cookbooks and culinary magazines.

There were two people who greatly influenced my love for food. The first was my Grandma Mary, who would always have me join her when she was in the kitchen. We would make many of the classic Italian peasant dishes. They were made with simple fresh ingredients, which happened to be plant-based. As my skills advanced, she taught me to make bread (her timeless recipe is included in this book). My tiny hands would become enveloped in five pounds of flour mixed with water, yeast, and other ingredients. I loved every moment of our time together. They are some of my fondest memories from my youth.

I found my second mentor at the age of six, while watching a new, ahead-of-its-time show called **The French Chef.** Each week I looked forward to Julia Child's demonstration with excitement and anticipation. This was where I learned about the science of cooking. Admittedly, there was nothing veg about her whatsoever. In fact, one of her more famous quotes was "If you're afraid of butter, use cream". But, not only did she have superb skills and extensive knowledge, she was also an inspirational teacher. She had an "if I can do it, so can you" attitude and a willingness to be perfectly imperfect. I was transported to her stage kitchen during every episode and was an eager student.

I remember the daily urgings from my parents to "eat your meat". I much preferred the wonderful array of both starches and veggies that were presented at meals. In reflection, I think that I was always meant to be vegan. I became a vegetarian in 1983, but continued to eat dairy and eggs (lacto-ovo vegetarian). I had completely bought into the "happy cow from California" marketing message as well as those meaningless catch phrases like free-range, vegetarian-fed, and antibiotic-free. Then I read a book in 2007 that forever changed my life. *Skinny Bitches*, by Freedman and Barnouin, shifted how I looked at both the dairy and the egg industries. I was astonished that it took me so long to learn about these atrocities. I had absolutely no idea! It was one of those "AHA!" moments when you know that your life will never be the same again.

So began my vegan journey. My newfound quest was not only creating original vegan recipes but

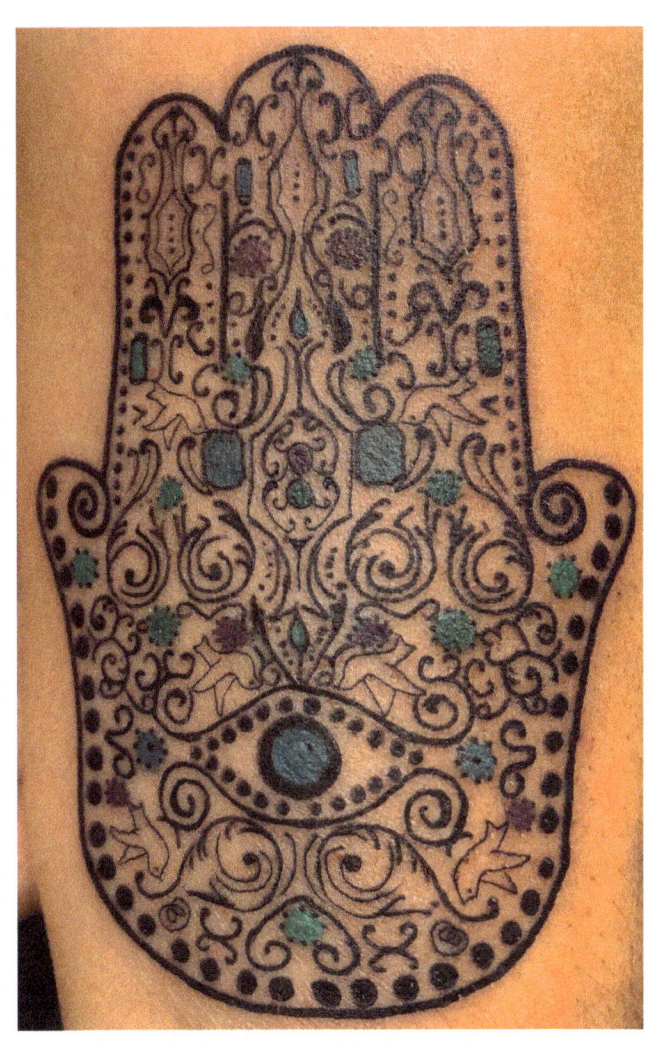

LINDA'S AHIMSA TATTOO COURTESY OF BRIAN WILSON, SCAPEGOAT TATTOO, PORTLAND, OREGON

also taking on the challenge of veganifying all of my favorite recipes that contained dairy, eggs, and meat. Over time I had amassed an extensive collection of my own unique recipes, as well as recipes from family and friends. I used these as inspiration to create veganified versions.

This is a vegan cookbook. When you read ingredients such as butter, milk, cheese, and eggs in a recipe, I am referring to their vegan versions. The chapter titled "Voorhis' Vegan Versions" contains a list of my favorite vegan brands. My list is certainly not exhaustive. Use it as a springboard for your own exploration into these products.

Within these pages, I share why I chose particular ingredients as well as tips and techniques I found helpful to ensure the gustatory pleasure of both vegans and omnivores alike. In addition to enjoying the recipes in this book, I hope it inspires you to adapt your own non-vegan recipes into vegan delectables.

Join me as, together, we celebrate the journey of becoming and being vegan.

In the Spirit of Ahimsa ...

Linda

*Veganification® is a Registered Trademark.

VEGANIFICATION®
TABLE OF CONTENTS

Introduction. X
Forward by JL Fields. 17

BREAKFAST ANY TIME
CHAPTER 1 19
Baked Stuffed French Toast 20
Tofu Scramble 21
Hash Brown Waffles. 22
Scones 23
Corn Muffins. 24
Award Winning Pumpkin Pecan Cranberry Muffins . . .25
Zucchini Muffins. 26
Muffins Made Simple. 27
Clotted Cream. 28
Lemon Curd 28
Prosecco Cherry Chia Jam 29
Spiked Maple Butter. 29
Buttermilk Biscuits with Country
"Red-eye" Mushroom Gravy. 30

APPETIZERS
CHAPTER 2 33
Amuse-Bouche Stuffed Potato Boats 34
Mini Roasted Red Pepper Quiche 35
Stuffed Mushrooms with an Herb Oil Drizzle. 36
Jalapeño Pepper Poppers 37
Devlish Eggs 38
Cheesy Rapini Spiral Pastries 39
Chichi Bean Spread
and Olive Tapenade on Crostini 40
Herbs de Provence Cashew Cheese Spread. 42

SAUCES, DRESSINGS AND CONDIMENTS
CHAPTER 3 43
Blender Hollandaise Sauce 44
Bolognese. 45
Tomato Gravy 46
Autumn Harvest Sauce 47
Peanut Sauce 48
Cashew Crema 48
Roasted Red Pepper Chimichurri. 48
Tomato Mango Lime Salsa 49
Parsley Cashew Dipping Sauce 49
Sweet & Sour Dipping Sauce 49
Indian Cilantro Chutney 50
Lemon-Chive Dressing 50
Maple Harissa Dressing 50
Horseradish Sauce 50

SOUPS
CHAPTER 4 51
Gazpacho 52
Creamy-Dreamy Cannellini Bean Soup 53
Minestra di Verdura e Riso. 54
Thai Corn Coconut Soup 55
Cauliflower & Macaroni Soup. 56
Black Bean Soup. 57
Butternut Squash Soup with Almond Cream & Spiced
Pumpkin Seeds. 58
Roasted Celery, Leek and Potato Soup with Bacon
and Gremolata Garnish 59

SALADS
CHAPTER 5 61

Grilled Caesar Salad with Buttermilk Dill Dressing
and Focaccia Crumble 62
Apple Fennel Salad. 62
Middle Eastern Farro Salad 64
Roasted Brussels Sprouts, Apples, Cranberries
and Walnut Salad 65
Creamy Pasta Primavera Salad 66
Potato Radicchio Salad with
Walnut/Kalamata Olive Pesto 67
Roasted Tomato & Grilled Corn
Chutney Quinoa Salad 68
Spanish Rice and Bean Salad 70

KEEPING IT UNDER WRAPS
CHAPTER 6 71

Dolmas (Dolmades) 72
Shumai Dumplings 74
Vegetable Cannelloni 75
Potato Cheese Pierogi 76
Chinese Egg-less Roll 78
Winter Rolls 80
Dessert Bollo with Crème Anglaise 81

THE MAIN EVENT
CHAPTER 7 83

Beef Wellington with Mushroom Spinach Stuffing
and Brown Gravy 84
Coquilles St. Jacques À La Provencale. 86
Molé Black Bean Stew
with Mango Sticky Rice 88
Cajun-Inspired Meatloaf 90
Tourlou – Greek Ratatouille 92
Chesapeake Bay Crabby Cakes 93
Eggplant and Rice Parmigiana 94
Butternut Squash Coconut
Curry Stew with Tempeh 95
Ethiopian-Spiced Roasted Root Vegetable Tart 96
Smoky Kale and Potato Casserole 98
Beatific Beet Burgers 99
Sourdough Pasta 100

YEAST DOUGHS
CHAPTER 8 103
English Muffins................................104
Cherry Orange Pecan Country Loaf.............105
Real-Deal Light and Airy Doughnuts...........106
Grandma Mary's Bread Loaf....................108
Focaccia.....................................110
Neopolitan-Style Pizza Dough.................112

SPECIALTY CAKES
CHAPTER 9 115
Limoncello Coconut Cake......................116
Italian Saffron Rice Torta...................119
Divinely-Decadent Chocolate Stout Cake.......120
Piña Colada Upside-down Cornmeal Cake........122
Indian Pistachio Date and Cardamom Cake......124
Carrot Cake With Cream Cheese Frosting.......126

FOR THE SWEET TOOTH
CHAPTER 10 127
Poached Pears With Meringue
And Chocolate Drizzle........................128
"I Am Not A Crook" Watergate Salad...........130
Blood Orange Tahini Cake.....................131
Black Bean Brownies..........................132
Pumpkin Pecan Chocolate Magic Bars...........133
Raw Key Lime Bars............................134
Grandma Mary's Pignoli Cookies...............135
Coconut Chocolate-Dipped Cookies.............136
Fruit Cake Cookies...........................137
Struffoli....................................138
Pizzelles....................................139
Never-Fail Buttercream Frosting..............140

VOORHIS' VEGAN VERSIONS...142
GLOSSARY.................144
INDEX....................147
ACKNOWLEDGMENTS..........155
ABOUT LINDA..............159
PHOTO CREDITS............161

FORWARD BY JL FIELDS

Confessions of a cookbook author: I've always felt a bit out of bounds when writing books. See, I'm a home cook. A vegan home cook who became an enthusiastic one by taking a class or two to ultimately launch a vegan cooking academy and teach future chefs in a university culinary program. It took a lot of work and study because it simply didn't come naturally to me.

There are other cooks and chefs who just have it: the instinct, the understanding, the ability to create beautiful food naturally.

Linda Voorhis is one of those culinary professionals.

The first time I sat in Linda's kitchen, I just watched her. Floating from pantry to cupboard to the counter, she effortlessly pulled together intoxicating dishes that boasted both simplicity in preparation and complexity in flavor. I knew she had a cookbook in her.

And you're holding it in your hands now.

Veganification® is both approachable (you can do this!) yet challenges the home cook to think and go big. Vegan cookbooks are easy to find and each has its special place and speaks to a certain audience. This is the book to use when you want to eat vegan and when you want to blow your family and friends away by preparing a delicious vegan feast. Linda delivers complex recipes – get ready to flex your culinary muscles! – by breaking them down, step by step so that you actually learn from the process. And that's no surprise because Linda is a Master Vegan Lifestyle Coach & Educator and her personal and professional vision is to make vegan eating, cooking, and living accessible.

Think of this book as a way to go next-level in your plant-based cooking. Make vegetables sing with subtle spices. Create drool-worthy sweets. Prepare salads that nourish your body and spirit. Most of all just sit back, relax, and enjoy the ride because Linda's guiding you the whole way.

JL FIELDS *Master Vegan Lifestyle Coach & Educator, culinary instructor, health coach, consulting chef, and author of numerous cookbooks, including Vegan Baking for Beginners, Fast & Easy Vegan Cookbook, Vegan Meal Prep, The Vegan Air Fryer, and Vegan Pressure Cooking*

CHAPTER 1

BREAKFAST ANY TIME

CROWD-PLEASING BREAKFAST DELECTABLES THAT AREN'T JUST FOR BREAKFAST ANY MORE.

Whether you are entertaining a crowd for a brunch or making breakfast for dinner, these easy yet elegant recipes will become some of your go-to's when you have a hankering for an A.M. (ante-meridian – before midday) meal regardless of the time of day or night.

BAKED STUFFED FRENCH TOAST

A perfect make-ahead offering that you can prep the day before and bake the next day just before serving. Excellent for a festive brunch or a lazy Sunday morning breakfast ... but heck, breakfast for dinner works for me just as well. Serve with warmed maple syrup or my spiked maple butter.

INGREDIENTS

- 1 loaf whole-grain bread, not sliced (gluten-free will work perfectly fine)
- 8 ounces cream cheese
- 1 cup fruit compote*1
- 2 cups buttermilk*2
- ½ cup silken tofu
- 3-4 tablespoons Vegan Egg or other egg substitute powder
- 1 tablespoon agave or maple syrup
- 2 teaspoons Kala Namak

OPTIONAL

- sugar for bruleé, fresh fruits that match the compote and/or slivered, toasted nuts, powdered confectioner's sugar.

SUBSTITUTIONS

- **Bread:** Swap out the bread with vegan croissants for a dressed-up version. Texas toast slices also work well.
- **Fruit Compote:** A high-qualtiy bar of dark chocolate, chopped and/or toasted nuts will knock your socks off as well.
- **Vegan Egg:** Use an equal amount of white whole wheat pastry flour or similar flour.

MAPLE BUTTER

To softened butter, whip an equal portion of real maple syrup. To kick it up, make it boozy by adding a splash (or two) of bourbon, anisette, Kalhua, or other favorite alcohol of your choice. For a "Shirley Temple" version, mix in a dash of cinnamon with a pinch of nutmeg, and cloves along with some minced candied ginger.

PROCEDURES

Lightly coat the inside of a 9"x13" casserole pan with a spritz of avocado oil or melted butter. Set aside.

Slice bread into 1½" thick slices, then cut in half on the diagonal. Slice a pocket into the cut side, ensuring that you don't cut all the way through the edges. Set aside.

If you are making homemade fruit compote, refer to Tips.*1 If you are using canned fruit compote, you might want to chop the fruit smaller so you can easily stuff it into the bread. I, personally, tend to stay away from canned fruit compote as they are typically loaded with way too much sugar. I prefer less sugar, more fruit taste. But that's me. You do what pleases you. In a bowl, mix together the cream cheese and fruit compote. Set aside.

In a blender, process the buttermilk, tofu, egg substitute, agave or maple syrup, and Kala namak until smooth. It should be slightly thinner than a pancake batter. If needed, adjust thickness by either adding a scant amount more of the buttermilk to thin it out or adding a scant amount more of silken tofu to thicken. Set aside.

Stuff the cream cheese compote mixture into the bread. Stuff it as much as you can without breaking the sides.

As you stuff each slice, arrange it in the casserole pan cut side tilted up slightly, then overlap the open stuffed side of the next slice over the first slice so that it fills gaps in the pan. Continue until you have all the slices stuffed and arranged in the casserole pan. Gently press them down, being careful not to have the stuffing come out.

Pour the buttermilk batter over the top of the stuffed slices, ensuring that you coat each one evenly.

Cover with plastic wrap, and park in refrigerator at least 8 hours, or overnight. This will allow the batter to soak into the French toast.

When ready, preheat oven to 350°F.

Place uncovered casserole into oven and bake for 30-35 minutes, or until the French toast is set and slightly browned on top.

If you'd like, as soon as you remove it from the oven, sprinkle with a scant amount of sugar, and bruleé the top.

OPTIONAL

Garnish with sliced fresh fruits that match the compote and slivered toasted almonds. If you didn't brulee the top, you can sprinkle with powdered sugar.

*1 **Fruit Compote:** In a saucepan, add 2 cups fresh or frozen fruit with 2 teaspoons agave, and 1 teaspoon orange or lemon juice. Bring to a boil, then reduce to simmer until the fruit is tender and beginning to break down. Remove from heat and allow to cool.

*2 **Buttermilk:** Add 1 teaspoon white cider vinegar to two cups milk. Stir vigorously, then allow to sit for ten minutes before using.

TOFU SCRAMBLE

It wouldn't be a vegan cookbook without a recipe for a tofu scramble. While I always encourage you to make recipes your own, tofu scramble is one of those recipes that never fails. It's perfect to use up those lone veggies that you need to do something with, or those leftovers that you would love to re-purpose. Have fun with this recipe … or make it as described. Either way, your choice. But enjoy, that is the key.

INGREDIENTS

- 12 baby bella mushrooms, sliced (chop larger mushrooms so they are bite-size slices)
- 6-7 asparagus stalks, sliced on the diagonal ⅛" thick
- 6-7 large radishes, sliced and diced (yes, radishes. I know you might be questioning me on this one; but please trust me, they work amazingly well in this dish.)
- 1 red pepper, diced
- 2 tablespoons avocado oil
- 1 large leek, washed and diced (do not use the tough green tops, save them for stock)
- 7-8 Brussels sprouts, shaved
- 2 pounds extra firm tofu, pressed to remove excess liquid, and crumbled
- ½ cup nutritional yeast, or more, depending on your liking
- 2 teaspoons turmeric
- 1½ teaspoons Kala Namak
- ¼ cup chickenless broth
- 1 teaspoon crushed fresh rosemary
- Fresh ground black pepper to taste

OPTIONAL

- hot sauce

PROCEDURES

In a large skillet, sauté the mushrooms, then set aside in a bowl.

In the same skillet, sauté the asparagus until tender. You can either spritz the pan with a scant amount of oil or use some broth. Set aside in the bowl with the mushrooms.

In the same skillet, sauté the radishes until tender. You can either spritz the pan with a scant amount of oil or use some broth. Set aside in the bowl with the other vegetables.

In the same skillet, sauté the pepper until tender. You can either spritz the pan with a scant amount of oil or use some broth. Set aside in the bowl with the other vegetables.

In the same skillet, sauté the leeks and Brussels sprouts in the avocado oil until tender and begin to caramelize.

Leaving the leeks and Brussels sprouts in the pan, add the tofu, nutritional yeast, turmeric, and Kala Namak, stirring to combine. Sauté until the tofu appears dry and begins to brown.

Add the parked vegetables to the pan and stir to combine and heat through.

Add the broth and rosemary and stir to combine until most of the broth is absorbed.

OPTIONAL

Add hot sauce or serve with hot sauce on the side

TIPS

Time saver – Prep the vegetables ahead of time and park in the refrigerator until ready to assemble the scramble.

HASH BROWN WAFFLES

You will be absolutely delighted with the flavor and texture of these hash browns, which are crispy on the outside with a soft interior.

INGREDIENTS

- 2 pounds Russet or Yukon Gold potatoes, peeled and shredded[*1]
- 3 tablespoons butter, melted
- 2 tablespoons nutritional yeast
- 2 teaspoons sea salt
- ½ teaspoon fresh ground black pepper

OPTIONAL

- For serving: sour cream or cashew cream with chives

PROCEDURES

Preheat a waffle iron on high heat.

Squeeze shredded potatoes in a clean dish towel to release excess water. This is an important step to ensure that the potatoes are dry enough to be able to crisp and not simply steam in the waffle iron.

In a large mixing bowl, mix the potatoes, butter, nutritional yeast, salt and pepper.

Depending on your waffle iron, you may or may not need to spritz the iron before adding the potatoes.

Scoop a ½-cup of the potato mixture into each waffle section.

Close the waffle iron and cook until hash browns are golden and tender, approximately 8-12 minutes, depending on how hot your iron becomes.

Repeat until all your batter is cooked. Place the finished hash browns in a warming drawer so they will remain hot and crispy but not continue to cook, sprinkling a touch of sea salt on each as you remove it from the iron.

You can prepare these ahead of time, and warm in a 325°F oven on wire racks for 5-7 minutes. Wrapped tightly, these are wonderful to make ahead and freeze. Don't defrost them before warming.

SERVING SUGGESTIONS

Dollop sour cream or cashew cream atop your "waffle" and sprinkle with chopped chives.

When you remove the hash brown from the iron, sprinkle with an herb mixture in addition to the salt.

Top with breaded chicken-less strips and mushroom gravy for a riff on Southern fried chicken and waffles.

[*1] I use Russet or Yukon Gold potatoes; however, you certainly could successfully swap them out for sweet potatoes. The Japanese sweet potatoes, which are quite starchy, do a fine job as a waffle iron hash brown. You just want to make sure that you select a starchy potato rather than a waxy, creamier potato.

SCONES

This is probably one of the most versatile recipes you'll ever need. Once you get the hang of it, which is really quite easy, you can use whatever add-ins you'd like for a completely different taste sensation, sweet or savory.

INGREDIENTS

- 2 cups white whole wheat pastry flour
- 3 tablespoons unrefined cane sugar
- 3 tablespoons Vegan Egg
- 1 tablespoon baking powder
- ½ teaspoon sea salt
- 6 tablespoons vegan butter, cold and cut in pieces
- 1¼ cup add-ins*1
- ⅓ cup plant-based milk (soy or coconut work best because of the fat content)
- Scant amount of bench flour

PROCEDURES

Pre-heat oven to 400°F and line a large sheet pan with parchment paper.

In a large mixing bowl, whisk together the flour, sugar, Vegan Egg, baking powder, and salt.

Cut the vegan butter into the dry ingredients (this step is easiest and you get the best results using clean fingers; but you can also use a pastry cutter, if you'd prefer)

Stir in the add-ins.

Combine the plant-based milk with the mixture until a loose dough forms. I like to use a wooden spoon for this step to mix and a rubber spatula to scrape off the dough from the spoon. Definitely only mix until it is mostly combined. Do not over mix.

On a very lightly-floured dough board, marble countertop, or similar, knead the dough for approximately one minute or until the dough comes together.

Roll out with a rolling pin to 1" thick, then cut the scones using a 2"-3" cookie cutter. Place scones on the prepared sheet pan.*2

Gently re-roll remaining dough and cut additional scones until all the dough is used. Reminder, however … the more you work the dough, the less tender the scone will be.

Bake for 20-25 mintures, or until golden on the outside and baked through on the inside.

Remove from oven when done and place scones on wire cooling rack until cooled.

OPTIONAL

Before putting in the oven to bake, sprinkle coarse sugar over the tops of the scones.

Make a glaze of confectioner's sugar and a liquid (water, bourbon, Grand Marnier, very loose pureed fruit water, etc.) and drizzle over the cooled scones before serving.

***1** For your add-ins: mini vegan chocolate chips, a combination of dried cranberries and walnuts, pistachios and dried apricots, apples and cheddar cheese. Here's where the sky's the limit. Have fun with this one. (Well, really, I do hope you have fun making all the recipes in this book; but this one is such a go-to recipe.)

***2** Another option is to roll out the dough on the parchment paper into a circle, then using a sharp knife, cut the dough into 8 pie-sliced shapes. Gently slide each scone out slightly so that there is room between each scone so they don't join back together during the baking process.

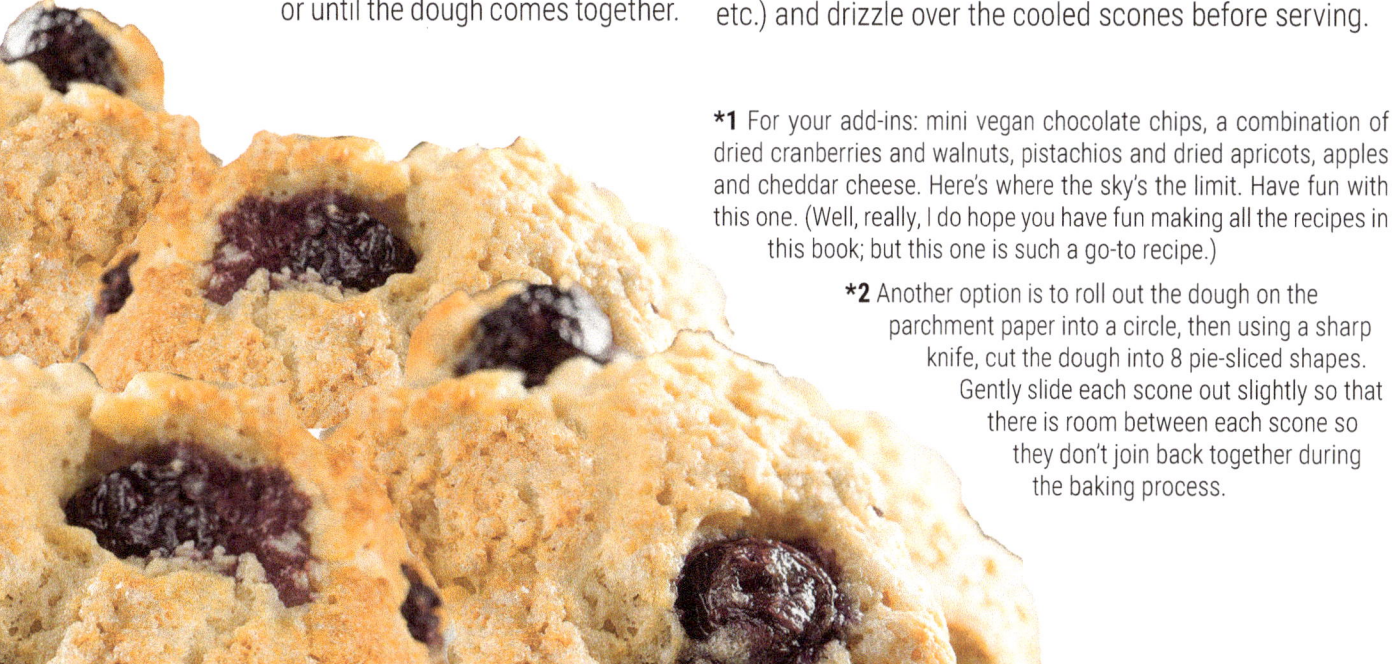

CORN MUFFINS

My favorite way to serve these muffins is to cut them into thirds lengthwise, then grill them. But that being said, they are perfect straight up as they are. They also make a stellar stuffing base. Served as an accompaniment to chili on a cold winter's night will warm not only your heart but also your tummy.

INGREDIENTS

- 3 cups yellow cornmeal
- 2 cups white whole wheat pastry flour
- 1½ cups unrefined sugar
- 2 tablespoons baking powder
- 1 teaspoon salt
- 2 cups milk
- ½ cup avocado oil
- 1½ cups JUST Egg

PROCEDURES

Preheat oven to 425°F.

Prepare muffin tin by spritzing lightly with avocado oil.

Mix dry ingredients together (cornmeal, flour, sugar, baking powder, and salt.

In large bowl, beat wet ingredients until well blended (milk, oil, and JUST Egg).

Add dry ingredients and stir until just blended. Do not over-mix.

If using a large muffin tin, use two standard-size ice cream scoops for each well. If using a regular-sized muffin tin, use one standard sized ice cream scoop per well.

Bake 25-35 minutes or until done for large muffins, and 18-22 for regular sized muffins. They will be done when a toothpick comes out clean. Do not over bake.

Remove from oven, and allow the muffins to cool in the pan for 10 minutes on a wire rack.

After 10 minutes, carefully remove the muffins from the pan and allow them to cool completely on a wire rack.

TIP

These muffins freeze well if you wrap them individually and securely.

AWARD WINNING PUMPKIN PECAN CRANBERRY MUFFINS

This recipe was the first recipe I ever entered in a Recipe Contest. Back on October 8, 2008, there was the South Jersey Pumpkin Festival. My son, Jason, his then-wife, and my 1st grandson, Jason, who at the time was five months old, came to visit me. There was a food contest at the Festival, which required that the main ingredient featured was pumpkin. I entered these muffins, which at the time, I was calling "Hurray for the Harvest Muffins". We had to submit enough of our entry so that the judges would be able to sample as well as some to go around for the crowd to try. Throughout the day, all I kept saying was that I wanted to win a ribbon. My son, on the other hand, was trying to be a voice of reason, saying that I should just be excited that I entered the contest, and my muffins were great, that I shouldn't expect to win the first time around. My retort to that was, "Well, if I didn't think they were good enough to win, then I shouldn't have entered them". Lo and behold, my muffins won 1st Place. I think my son squealed louder and jumped higher than even I did, as he was yelling, "That's my Mom! That's my Mom!" I not only got the blue ribbon, which was really all I cared about; but I also received a lovely set of ceramic mixing bowls, that I still use to this day in fond remembrance. So, needless to say, it is a wonderful memory, and I got to tell my son, "I told you so." The recipe back then was vegetarian, and I have since tweaked it so it is now vegan.

INGREDIENTS

- 2½ cups white whole wheat pastry flour
- 2¼ teaspoons cinnamon
- 1½ teaspoons baking soda
- ½ teaspoon salt
- ¼ teaspoon nutmeg
- ¼ teaspoon allspice
- ¼ teaspoon ground cloves
- 10-oz bag fresh cranberries
- 1 cup pecans, chopped
- 2 cups unrefined cane sugar
- 1¼ cups cooked pureed pumpkin
- ½ cup JUST Egg
- ⅓ cup avocado oil

PROCEDURES

Preheat oven to 350°F

Prepare a large muffin tin by lightly spritzing it with oil.

In a bowl, whisk the dry ingredients together: flour, cinnamon, baking soda, salt, nutmeg, allspice, and cloves.

Add the cranberries and pecans to the dry ingredients, and stir to combine. [*1]

In a large bowl, beat together the sugar, pumpkin, egg substitute, and oil until well blended.

Add the dry ingredients to the bowl of wet ingredients. Stir until just combined.

Using a standard ice cream scoop, dollop two scoops into each muffin well. You should get 11 large muffins. [*2]

Bake 30-35 minutes or until a toothpick comes out clean. [*2]

[*1] When you mix the add-ins to the dry ingredients, it helps to coat them, which stops them from floating down to the bottom of your muffins, keeping them scattered throughout the entire muffin.

[*2] If you are using a standard size muffin tin, only put one scoop into each muffin well, and adjust the baking time to 18-22 minutes, or until a toothpick comes out clean.

ZUCCHINI MUFFINS

Recently, I started my own sourdough starter. It hasn't been without its challenges; but I've been really enjoying the learning curve. Now, that being said, how many loaves of sourdough bread can one person bake? My sourdough starter's name is MJ, short for Mary Josephine, named in honor of the Immaculate Conception since MJ gets fed and then gives birth to bread or some other baked good.

I've been working on coming up with different ideas for the sourdough discard; and came up with this Zucchini Muffin recipe. While my sourdough skills are not yet quite ready for primetime, this recipe just blew me away when it came out of the oven. So, it was a last minute addition to this cookbook. I hope you enjoy it as much as I enjoyed creating it.

INGREDIENTS

- 3⅓ cups white whole wheat pastry flour
- 2 teaspoons cinnamon
- 1 teaspoon baking soda
- 1 teaspoon baking powder
- ½ teaspoon salt
- ⅛ teaspoon nutmeg
- ⅛ teaspoon ground ginger
- Pinch of ground allspice
- Pinch of ground cloves
- 2 cups unrefined cane sugar
- 1½ cups sourdough starter discard
- ½ cup JUST Egg
- ⅓ cup avocado oil
- 1½ teaspoons vanilla
- 3 cups shredded zucchini*1

PROCEDURES

Preheat oven to 350°F

Prepare a large muffin tin by lightly spritzing it with oil.

In a bowl, whisk the dry ingredients together: flour, cinnamon, baking soda, baking powder, salt, nutmeg, ginger, allspice, and cloves. Set aside.

In a large mixing bowl and using a hand mixer or whisk, beat together the sugar, sourdough discard, egg substitute, oil, and vanilla until well blended.

Fold in the zucchini until well combined.

Add the dry ingredients to the wet ingredients in three stages, folding in between each addition until the ingredients are just combined.

Using a standard ice cream scoop, dollop two scoops into each muffin well. You should get 12 large muffins.*2

Bake 30-35 minutes or until a toothpick comes out clean.*2

*1 Three cups is equal to approximately three small zucchinis when shredded. Do not pack the zucchini to measure it out. Simply shred it and measure, without squeezing out excess moisture.

*2 If you are using a standard size muffin tin, only put one scoop into each muffin well, and adjust the baking time to 18-22 minutes, or until a toothpick comes out clean.

MUFFINS MADE SIMPLE

This is my basic go-to recipe for making muffins. The add-ins that you opt for are what make it special and yours. Just remember, dry ingredients are mixed in a large mixing bowl. Wet ingredients, which include granulated sugar, are whisked in a separate bowl, and then incorporated into the dry ingredients.

INGREDIENTS

- 3½ cups white whole wheat pastry flour
- 1 cup unrefined cane sugar
- 5 teaspoons baking powder
- 1½ teaspoons salt
- 1½ cups milk (soy or coconut preferred)
- ⅔ cup avocado oil
- 4 tablespoons VeganEgg whisked into ½ up water; or ½ cup JUST Egg
- 1 teaspoon vanilla (or other flavoring)
- At least 1 cup of blueberries, cherries, chocolate chips, and/or nuts, etc.

PROCEDURES

Preheat oven to 400°F.

Prepare your muffin tins by lightly spritzing with avocado oil.

Whisk together flour, sugar, baking powder and salt in a large mixing bowl.

Gently toss the blueberries into the flour mixture.

In a small bowl, whisk together the milk, oil, egg substitute, and vanilla until well blended.

Pour wet ingredients into dry ingredients. Stir until just blended. Do not over-mix.

If using a standard size muffin tin and using a standard-size ice cream scoop, dollop one scoop into each well. If using the baking tins that makes large muffins, dollop two scoops into each well.

Bake 25-35 minutes, or until done (a toothpick comes out clean) for large muffins (two scoops) and 17-19 minutes for medium-sized muffins (1 scoop).

Allow muffins to cool 10-15 minutes in pan on wire rack before removing from the muffin tin, then allow them to cool completely on the wire rack.

TIPS

The reason you want to toss your add-ins into the dry ingredients is because the flour mixture will coat the add-ins, thus stopping them from dropping down to the bottom of the muffins.

Swap out ½ cup of the flour for ¾ cup raw cocoa powder for a chocolate muffin. Add 2 tablespoons additional sugar for a sweeter muffin. For a more chocolatey muffin, add in ⅓ cup shaved or grated dark chocolate bar and 2 teaspoons instant espresso.

Make a crumble to top the muffins before baking.

I have a myriad of ice cream scoops that I use for baking. Depending on the muffin tin you are using, choose a scoop that will fill the tin to approximately ⅔ full. You will not only have perfectly sized muffins but also evenly-baked muffins.

CLOTTED CREAM

This British spread is typically served alongside scones with tea. It's incredibly easy to throw together and will have you wondering how you've ever eaten a scone or breakfast muffin without it.

INGREDIENTS

- 1.8 ounces cultured butter
- 2.6 ounces rice or tapioca flour
- 3-5 tablespoons sweetened condensed coconut milk

PROCEDURES

Using either a stand mixer or portable hand mixer, whip the butter and flour together until you have a buttercream texture. Start off on the lowest speed lest you might become Snow White from the flour jumping out of the bowl. Gradually increase speed as mixture becomes homogenous.

While it continues to whip, slowly add the sweetened condensed milk until you have a light, fluffy texture that resembles clotted cream.

You can use immediately but best served when chilled for several hours, then left out to stand for 10-15 minutes before diving in.

Will last in the refrigerator for up to several days if covered and sealed well.

LEMON CURD

Classically served during an elegant British brunch or afternoon tea, lemon curd is typically lemons with lots eggs yolks and butter. But not today. I've veganified this masterpiece. Dolloped atop a scone, muffin, or French Toast, this is a winner. Although sweet, you can bring this to your dinner table to garnish steamed broccoli or a vegetable medley as well.

INGREDIENTS

- 6 large organic lemons, zested and juiced, separated
- 1½ cups unrefined cane sugar
- 2 tablespoons Vegan Egg mixed in ½ cup water
- ½ cup butter

PROCEDURES

In a small bowl, rub together the lemon zest and sugar to scent the sugar and release the oils from the zest into the sugar.

Add all the ingredients into a heavy-bottomed, medium-sized saucepan.

Over medium-low heat, stir continuously so the butter melts and the ingredients combine to create a homogenous viscous liquid.

Continue stirring and cooking until the mixture thickens and begins to coat the spoon, approximately 12-15 minutes.

Pour the curd into a glass bowl and apply plastic wrap or parchment paper directly onto the top of the curd so a crust will not form.

Allow the curd to cool to room temperature, cover to seal the bowl, and refrigerate at least 6-8 hours before serving.

PROSECCO CHERRY CHIA JAM

This jam is kicked-up-a-notch and made more flavorful and sophisticated with the use of Prosecco.

INGREDIENTS
- 1 cup frozen or fresh cherries, chopped (thawed if frozen)
- 2½ tablespoons sugar
- 2½ tablespoons Prosecco
- 1 tablespoon whole plus 1 teaspoon ground chia seeds
- 1 teaspoon lemon zest

PROCEDURES

Whisk together all ingredients in a saucepan.

Over medium-low heat, continue whisking and bring to a simmer.

Continue cooking and whisking for an additional 3-4 minutes, or until jam thickens.

Remove from heat and allow to cool before packing in a glass jar.

Refrigerate at least 3-4 hours before using to allow jam to set up.

OPTIONS

Swap out the cherries for peaches, blueberries, raspberries, or mango.

If you prefer, swap out the Prosecco with fruit juice.

SPIKED MAPLE BUTTER

Add elegance to your breakfast table by serving this butter. I like to use silicone chocolate molds to form pats of this butter and serve them on a small fancy plate.

INGREDIENTS
- ¾ cup Miyoko's cultured butter
- ½ cup maple syrup
- 2 tablespoons rum, applejack, Grand Marnier, Kahlua, or other similar liquor
- Zest from one orange, optional

PROCEDURES

Allow the butter to sit on the counter in a mixing bowl until soft, approximately ½-hour.

Using a hand mixer, immersion blender or wire whisk, combine all ingredients until homogenous.

Spoon butter into a lovely serving bowl or silicone mold, and smooth out the top. Cover with plastic wrap and refrigerate until ready to serve. Pop out butter pats if you used the silicone mold.

Keep chilled until 10 minutes before serving.

You can serve this as a butter, or gently warm until the butter becomes liquid, and serve in a gravy boat. You will need to whisk the butter to keep it from separating occasionally if it is going to sit out for a short while.

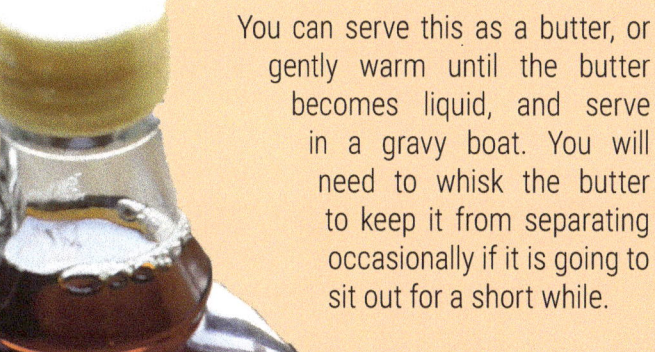

BUTTERMILK BISCUITS WITH COUNTRY "RED-EYE" MUSHROOM GRAVY

BISCUITS
INGREDIENTS

- 2½ cups white whole wheat pastry flour
- 1 tablespoon baking powder
- ½ teaspoon baking soda
- ⅛ teaspoon sea salt
- 4 heaping tablespoons Miyoko's cultured vegan butter (chilled & cubed)
- 1 cup buttermilk*1

PROCEDURES

Preheat oven to 425°F.

In a large mixing bowl, whisk together the flour, baking powder, baking soda, and salt.

To cut the butter into the flour, you'll get the best results if you dump the flour mixture onto a marble or granite slab first or use a stainless steel bowl that you've had in the freezer for ½-hour prior to use.

Cut the cold butter into the flour mixture (here you can use a pastry blender or fork, but I prefer the old-fashion method of using my hands. You'll need to work quickly as you don't want the warmth of your hands to melt the butter. I have a bowl of ice water nearby that I use to dip my hands in, then dry my hands well, and work quickly.) It is important to not overwork this step. You want some pea-size balls and crumbly flour. Not all the flour will be combined at this point.

Add in the buttermilk, again working quickly to make a dough. The dough should be able to be rolled into a ball, and feel slightly tacky, but not sticky. Depending on your flour, you might need to add a little extra flour.

Sprinkle some bench flour on a clean marble or granite surface. Quickly roll it out (here again, it will work best if you have your rolling pin parked in the freezer for ½-hour prior to use), then fold it over itself, quickly roll it out, then fold it over itself again. If at any time the dough is getting warm, place the slab in the refrigerator for 5 minutes to re-chill.

Roll out to ¾" thick. Using a 2½" cookie cutter (first dipping the cookie cutter into flour so that biscuits easily come out of the cutter), cut out the biscuits.

Place biscuits on a baking sheet lined with parchment paper.

Optional: Brush with some buttermilk or melted butter.

Bake in oven for 15-18 minutes.

*1 Buttermilk: Now you can certainly do the quick buttermilk, which is one tablespoon lemon juice or white vinegar to one cup milk. Stir vigorously, then allow it to sit for 10 minutes. You will have decent results. But if you really want this recipe to shine, I'd suggest that you make your own buttermilk. My go-to recipe for buttermilk can be found in the *The Non-Dairy Evolution Cookbook*, by Skye Michael Conroy, ©2014, Page 34.

TIPS

Both the biscuits and gravy can be made in advance and parked in the refrigerator. In fact, both freeze well if you have leftovers or want to plan ahead. Defrost both in the refrigerator. Warm the biscuits in a low 250°F oven for 10 minutes while you gently warm the gravy.

COUNTRY "RED-EYE" MUSHROOM GRAVY

INGREDIENTS

- 8-10 baby bella mushrooms, coarsely chopped
- 4 Breakfast Sausages, chopped
- 5 tablespoons butter
- 7 tablespoons white whole wheat pastry flour or gluten-free flour
- ¾ teaspoon poultry seasoning
- ¼ teaspoon nutmeg
- ¼ cup strong coffee or espresso
- 3¾ cups soy milk
- 1 teaspoon sea salt
- ½ teaspoon fresh ground white pepper

PROCEDURES

In large saucepan, sweat the mushrooms until soft and tender and they have exuded their juices.

Add the breakfast sausage, and sauté until slightly browned.

Add the butter and flour, stir to combine and make a roux. Cook, stirring constantly, for 2 minutes to cook the flour. Do not allow the roux to brown.

Add the poultry seasoning and nutmeg, whisking only to combine.

Whisk in the coffee, and soy milk, whisking constantly so you don't have any lumps.

Stir constantly until the gravy thickens.

Season with sea salt and pepper.

CHAPTER 2

APPETIZERS

ENTICING HORS D'OEUVRES THAT WILL BEGUILE AND TITILLATE ALL YOUR SENSES.

These tasty crowd pleasers are perfect for an intimate cocktail party or as the first course to set the stage for a multi-course dinner extravaganza.

AMUSE-BOUCHE STUFFED POTATO BOATS

Bite-sized potatoes stuffed with a sausage spinach stuffing.
You won't be able to stop popping these morsels into your mouth.

INGREDIENTS

- 2 pounds mini red bliss potatoes, cut in half
- 1 10-ounce package frozen spinach, defrosted
- 1½ tablespoons avocado oil
- ⅓ cup minced onion
- 3 cloves garlic, minced
- 4 Italian Sausage links
- ⅓ cup nutritional yeast
- ⅓ cup Shredded Parmesan Cheese
- Sea Salt and fresh ground black pepper to taste

PROCEDURES

Preheat your oven to 450°F with a large cookie sheet in the oven.

In a bowl, toss the potatoes with the oil and season with salt and pepper.

Remove the cookie sheet from the oven, being careful with it because it will be scorching hot. Quickly put the potatoes on the cookie sheet, and return to oven.

Roast the potatoes for 20 minutes, or until just fork-tender. You do not want to overcook them. In fact, you can slightly undercook them as they will continue to cook when you remove them from the oven.

As soon as you remove the potatoes from the oven, transfer them to a cool cookie sheet or serving platter.

Using a small paring knife or melon scoop, scoop out a small amount of the potato. Set aside the potato that you scoop out as you will use it for the stuffing.

Place the spinach in a clean dish towel, and squeeze to remove the excess moisture. If the spinach isn't chopped, go ahead and chop it. Set aside.

In a large skillet, sauté the onions in the oil until translucent, approximately 10 minutes.

Add the garlic, and sauté until the garlic is fragrant.

If the sausage has a casing, remove it from the casing. Add the sausage to the skillet, breaking it up as you sauté it with the onions and garlic.

When it is browned, add the spinach, and stir to combine.

Remove from heat and pour mixture into a bowl. Allow it to cool for 10-15 minutes.

Add the reserved potatoes, nutritional yeast, cheese, salt and black pepper. If the mixture is too dry to form, add a scant amount of water.

Using a spoon, gather approximately a tablespoon and roll into a ball, then press it onto the top of potato, pressing it into the well and then smoothing it out to the edges of the potato, leaving it mounded somewhat in the center.

Continue this process until you have all the potatoes stuffed.

At this point, you can park them in the refrigerator for baking at a later time, if you'd like.

To bake, preheat oven to 375°F.

Optional, lightly spritz the potato boats with oil to help them brown and stay moist.

Bake for 15-18 minutes, or until potato boats are warmed through and the stuffing has formed a light crust.

Serve hot or at room temperature.

SERVING OPTIONS

Serve with a bowl of Chimichurri or Cilantro Chutney on the side.

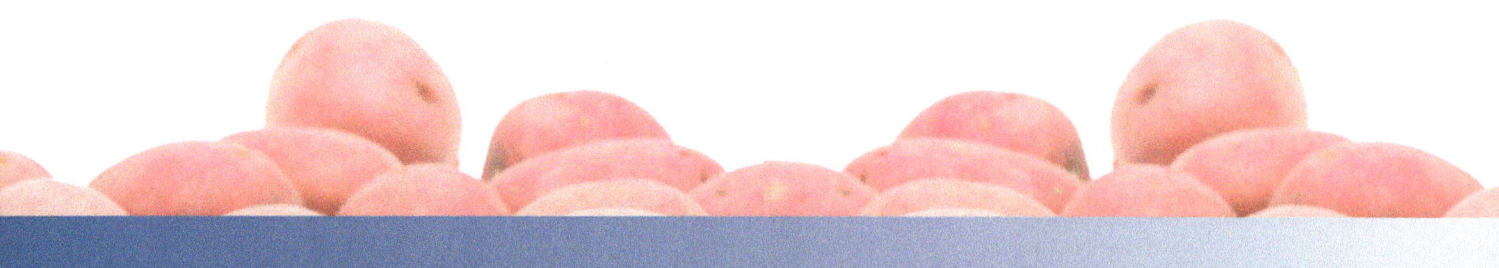

MINI ROASTED RED PEPPER QUICHE

These mini quiche are made with aquafaba in mini cupcake tins lined with phyllo pastry dough. No one will ever guess that, rather than using eggs, you used that liquid from a can of garbanzo beans that we used to toss down the kitchen drain but that now has a fancy-smanzy ingredient name, Aquafaba (Latin for "bean water").

INGREDIENTS

- 1 package whole wheat phyllo dough sheets
- ¼ cup olive oil or melted butter
- ¾ cup raw cashew pieces
- ¾ cup yogurt, plain and unsweetened*1
- 2 fifteen-ounce jars roasted red peppers, drained and the peppers patted dry
- ¾ cup aquafaba
- ¼ teaspoon cream of tartar
- 2 tablespoons coconut oil, melted and at room temperature
- ½ cup plus 1 tablespoon almond flour or oat flour
- 2 tablespoons nutritional yeast
- 1 teaspoon sea salt
- ¼ teaspoon turmeric
- ¼ teaspoon garlic powder
- ¼ teaspoon ground black pepper

PROCEDURES

Preheat oven to 350°F.

Unwrap phyllo sheets and park between two barely damp clean dish towels. This will prevent the sheets from drying out and cracking while working with them. You'll need to work rather quickly in prepping the sheets as they do have a tendency to dry out and crack.

On a clean workspace (you could use a piece of waxed paper or parchment for this step, but you'll need to ensure that you don't include it in your crust layer), carefully lay down one sheet of phyllo dough so that it doesn't tear, then brush with olive oil. Repeat this step 6 times, so that you have six layers of stacked phyllo dough.

Cut your layered sheets into 24 equal pieces.

Using a mini-muffin pan, line each muffin well with one set of phyllo squares, ensuring that you have pressed it against the bottom and sides. An easy way to do this as well as to ensure that you press it into the crease at the bottom is to use your fingertip (if you don't have long nails) or the top end of a chop stick. You will need to pinch some of the phyllo together as you push it into the well to help it fit snugly into each well.

Dock (prick) the bottoms and sides of the phyllo cups. Cover with a damp clean dish towel to avoid the phyllo from drying out while you prepare the filling.

To prepare the quiche filling, begin by combining the cashews & yogurt in a blender and blend until smooth. Set aside.

Chop the roasted red peppers into small dices. Set aside.

In a stand mixer, add the aquafaba and cream of tartar. Whip for five minutes at medium speed, then increase to high, continuing to whip for additional 11 to 13 minutes, until stiff peaks are formed.

Slowly add the coconut oil into the whipped aquafaba until blended, approximately one minute.

In a large mixing bowl, whisk together the dry ingredients until well combined (flour, nutritional yeast, salt, turmeric, garlic powder, and black pepper).

Add the nut/yogurt mixture to the dry ingredients, and whisk until well combined.

Add ⅓ of the aquafaba meringue to the bowl, gently folding it in with a spatula until combined, being careful not to deflate the meringue.

Add the second ⅓ of the aquafaba meringue to the bowl, gently folding in until barely combined, again being careful not to deflate the meringue.

Add the third ⅓ of the aquafaba to the bowl, gently folding in until barely combined, yet again being careful not to deflate the meringue.

Sprinkle one-half of the roasted red peppers on the bottom of the phyllo crusts.

Fill your mini phyllo cups ⅔ full, then sprinkle the remaining roasted red peppers on the top of the filling.

Bake for 25 minutes or until toothpick comes out clean.

Serve warm or room temperature.

*1 If the yogurt is more runny than it is solid; put some cheesecloth in a strainer, then pour the yogurt into the strainer, which is set over a bowl. Set in the refrigerator for at least several hours, or overnight, until the yogurt has released its extra water and is more thickly set.

STUFFED MUSHROOMS WITH AN HERB OIL DRIZZLE

I absolutely adore the meatiness of baby bella mushrooms.

INGREDIENTS

- 4 corn muffins, broken into small pieces and dried out in a warm oven*[1]
- 24 stuffing mushrooms, preferably baby bellas, but button will work
- ¼ cup minced onions
- ¼ cup minced shallots
- ¼ cup minced celery
- 2 tablespoons olive oil, separated
- 1 teaspoon minced fresh thyme or marjoram
- ¼ teaspoon crushed black pepper
- ⅛ teaspoon minced rosemary
- ⅛ teaspoon sage
- 1½ teaspoons black truffle sea salt
- ½ cup vegetable broth, warmed
- Herbed Olive Oil (recipe on next page)

PROCEDURES

Preheat oven to 400°F.

Lightly crumble dried corn muffins, leaving texture and larger-sized crumbs. Park them in a large mixing bowl.

Using a mushroom brush or slightly damp clean dish towel, wipe the mushrooms to remove any soil.

Separate the stems from the caps and set the caps aside.

Mince the stems, and set them aside.

In sauté pan, add 1 tablespoon oil, add the onions, shallots, and celery. Sauté until translucent*[2].

Add the minced mushrooms and cook until mushrooms are soft.

Add thyme, black pepper, rosemary, and sage, and continue cooking until fragrant, but do not burn. It should take another thirty seconds to one minute. Remove from heat, and set aside.

Add the duxelle mixture to the crumbled corn muffins along with black truffle sea salt, and gently toss to combine.

Starting with ¼ cup, toss the vegetable broth into the mixture. Depending on how dry the muffins are, you will need to add some or all of the additional vegetable broth. You do not want the mixture to be saturated, you just want it damp and slightly moist but with some parts still crunchy as the moisture from the mushroom will help soften the rest during the cooking process.

Stuff each mushroom cap with stuffing and place on a parchment-lined cookie sheet.*[3]

Using the remaining one tablespoon of olive oil, lightly brush each mushroom and stuffing. This aids the browning process during cooking.

Place mushrooms in a single layer on a cookie sheet.

Bake for 20-25 minutes, until mushrooms are softened and the stuffing has turned slightly golden brown.

Serve warm for best flavor, but room temperature works just as well. Have the herbed olive oil set alongside the mushrooms in a drizzle bottle or small dish with mini ladle.

HERBED OLIVE OIL

INGREDIENTS
- ½ cup olive oil
- 2 garlic cloves, minced
- 1 very small sprig rosemary
- 2 sage leaves
- ¼ teaspoon black truffle sea salt

PROCEDURES
In a small saucepan, warm the olive oil with the garlic on low until fragrant. Do not allow the garlic to take on any color.

Remove from heat and add the rosemary and sage.

Cover and allow the oil to steep with the garlic and herbs until completely cooled.

Strain and stir in the salt.

*1 You can make my Corn Muffin recipe, that you'll find in the "Breakfast Anytime" section. You can also use gluten-free bread instead of the corn muffins and have a delicious appetizer; however, it will definitely change up the flavor. You could retain some of the corn flavor by pureeing some corn kernels, mixing the puree with the bread, and reducing the amount of liquid.

*2 Sautéing minced mushrooms, onions, and shallots, which will be used as a stuffing, is called a "duxelle" (fancy French term, right?). So, when you're serving these tasty delights to your guests, be sure to throw out this term when describing your Hors D'oeuvres.

*3 To ensure that your duxelle is equal in all the mushroom caps, you can use a small ice cream scoop (1 or 2 tablespoons, depending on the size of the mushroom caps).

JALAPEÑO PEPPER POPPERS

Diminutive peppers, stuffed with a rice and herb stuffing, then roasted to perfection.

INGREDIENTS
- ½ cup fresh herbs (any single or combination of parsley, cilantro, mint, tarragon, basil, dill)
- 1⅛ cups unchicken broth
- ⅛ teaspoon sea salt
- ¼ cup onions, minced
- 2 teaspoons olive oil
- 2 cloves garlic, minced
- ½ cup brown basmati rice
- ¼ cup sour cream
- ½ cup shredded cheddar cheese, separated
- 1 dozen jalapeño peppers*1 sliced in half lengthwise
- 1 small bag of kettle-cooked potato chips, crushed into small bits

PROCEDURES
Preheat oven to 400°F.

Line two large cookie sheets with parchment paper. Set aside.

In a blender, process the herbs, broth, and sea salt until well blended. Set aside.

In a sauce pan that has a lid, sauté the onions in the oil on medium heat until caramelized, approximately 15 minutes.

Add the garlic, and sauté until the garlic is fragrant.

Add the rice and herb/broth mixture.

Bring to a boil, then reduce to simmer for 50 minutes, or until the rice is tender and the liquid is absorbed. Be careful not to scorch the herbs by continuing to cook the rice when the liquid is absorbed.

Remove from heat, turn into a mixing bowl, and allow to cool.

Stir in the sour cream and ¼ cup of the cheddar cheese.

Stuff the mixture into the jalapeno halves, placing them on the cookie sheet. Continue until you have all the peppers stuffed.

Sprinkle the remaining cheese and then the potato chips on the top of the stuffing.

Bake for 18-20 minutes.

Serve warm or at room temperature.

*1 If you are adverse to the capsaicin heat from the jalapenos, you can swap them out for sweet peppers.

DEVLISH EGGS

These vegan delights will fool even your most discerning omnivore. I made these once for a vegetarian potluck, where they had two separate tables set up, one for vegetarian options (made with dairy and/or eggs), and one for vegan options. So, these being vegan, I placed them on the vegan table. Twice during the potluck, someone moved them over to the vegetarian table, until I finally made an announcement that they were, in fact, vegan.

INGREDIENTS

EGG WHITES

- 2 cups soy or almond milk,[*1] unsweetened and plain
- 1 tablespoon agar agar
- ¼ teaspoon kala namak

DEVILED EGG YOLK

- 1 15-ounce can garbanzo beans, drained (reserve aquafaba for another use)
- ⅓ to ½ cup mayonnaise (can substitute ½ very ripe medium-sized avocado)
- 2 tablespoons nutritional yeast
- 3 teaspoons lemon juice
- 2 teaspoons Dijon mustard or ½ teaspoon mustard powder
- 1 teaspoon curry powder
- ½ teaspoon kala namak
- White pepper, freshly ground to taste

PROCEDURES

In saucepan, combine all ingredients for the egg whites, whisking well to combine.

Over slightly higher than medium heat, bring the mixture to a boil, whisking constantly.

Continue to stir for one additional minute.

Remove from heat and pour into egg molds.

Refrigerate for at least 30 minutes to allow 'eggs' to set.

In small food processor bowl, combine all egg yolk ingredients until well combined.

If you have a pastry bag, fit it with a medium/large star tip, then fill the bag with the egg yolk mixture.

To assemble the devilish eggs, remove a scant rounded amount of the white to create the egg yolk well in the wider side of the egg white.[*2]

Pipe the deviled egg yolk mixture into the well. If you aren't using a pastry bag, you can scoop the egg yolk mixture into the well. You want the egg yolk mixture to create a mound over the egg white.

Refrigerate at least 30 minutes; and keep refrigerated until ready to serve.

OPTIONAL

Sprinkle deviled eggs with minced chives and/or paprika to garnish.

***1** My preference is the soy milk because it is typically more viscous than the almond milk; but the almond milk also works well. If you are opting to use the almond milk, you might want to add a pinch more agar agar.

***2** If you have a very small melon scoop or an espresso spoon, it would help make this task much easier.

CHEESY RAPINI SPIRAL PASTRIES

Garlic-infused broccoli rabe and cheese rolled in puff pastry and baked into delectable spirals for the perfect flavor-popping tidbit.

INGREDIENTS

- 1 head broccoli rabe
- 1 tablespoon avocado oil
- 4 cloves garlic, minced
- ¼ cup unchicken broth, plus extra if needed
- ⅓ cup cream cheese
- ¼ cup shredded Parmesan cheese
- ¼ cup shredded mozzarella cheese
- 2 tablespoons nutritional yeast
- 1 package puff pastry, defrosted[*1]

PROCEDURES

Preheat oven to 375°F.

Line two large cookie sheets with parchment paper. Set aside.

Place the broccoli rabe in a food processor. Pulse to coarsely mince the broccoli robe. Be careful to not over process as you do not want a paste. You still want texture. Set aside.

In a large skillet, sauté the garlic in the oil until just fragrant. Add the broccoli rabe and unchicken broth. Stir to combine, then sauté until the broccoli rabe is cooked through and soft, and the broth is evaporated. If the broth evaporates before the broccoli rabe is cooked, add a scant amount.

Remove from heat and pour the broccoli rabe into a mixing bowl. Allow to cool for 10-15 minutes.

Add the cream cheese, Parmesan cheese, mozzarella, and nutritional yeast. Stir to combine well.

Open the puff pastry package. On a lightly-floured surface and using a rolling pin, gently roll the pastry to an 11"x14" rectangle. You want the rectangle to be 14" left to right and the 11" being front to back.

Spread the filling evenly over the puff pastry, leaving a ½" border on the long end of the pastry that is opposite to you. This will ensure that you are able to seal the pastry after rolling it up without the filling being in the way of accomplishing this task.

Lightly brush the border with a touch of water. You can also use a touch of an egg substitute if you have it readily available.

Working front to back, carefully roll the puff pastry so that it is slightly taught but not tight. When you get to the back end, place the roll seam side down to seal the dough.

At this point, it is helpful if you can place this roll on a sheet pan and park in the refrigerator for 20-25 minutes. This will help the puff pastry to become slightly stiff so that it is easier to cut. It's not a necessary step, but is definitely one that you will find beneficial.

Remove the roll from the refrigerator and cut ¼" wheels. As you cut them, please them on cookie sheets, leaving at least 1" between the wheels.

Bake for 10-12 minutes, or until the puff pastry is golden brown and baked through.

Remove from oven, then slide the parchment paper with the wheels onto wire racks so they cool.

Serve warm or at room temperature.

*1 Pepperidge Farm Puff Pastry is accidentally vegan.

CHICHI BEAN SPREAD AND OLIVE TAPENADE ON CROSTINI

Now that you have the liquid from the can of garbanzo beans taken care of, what to do with the leftover garbanzo beans (isn't it rather funny that we are talking about the beans as the leftover ingredient rather than the liquid?) Well, you could always make a ChiChi bean salad by adding chopped celery, some fresh herbs, and a vinaigrette dressing; but we are talking Hor D'oeuvres here, so that wouldn't work as a finger food item. This is an easy recipe that you can prepare all components up to several days in advance and assemble just before serving.

INGREDIENTS
- Crostini (recipe on next page)
- Tapenade Spread (recipe on next page)
- ChiChi Bean Spread (recipe below)
- 48 parsley or cilantro leaves[*1]

PROCEDURES
When ready to assemble, take ChiChi Bean Spread out and let sit at room temperature for ½-hour to slightly soften. Using a pastry bag with a medium-large scalloped tip, fill the bag with the spread.

Strain the oil that you prepped for the crostini, then lightly brush each crostini piece with a touch of the flavored olive oil.

Spread a small amount of the olive tapenade on top of each crostini.

Top the crostini with a dollop of the ChiChi Bean Spread. You can use a pastry bag for this step, which would help to not only avoid messing up the tapenade but will also add a decorative touch to the crostini.

Adorn with a fresh parsley or fresh cilantro leaf, depending on which herb you used in your tapenade.

CHICHI BEAN SPREAD

INGREDIENTS
- 2 cans drained garbanzo beans[*4]
- 4 tablespoons tahini
- 4 teaspoons sesame seed oil
- ¾ teaspoon sea salt
- ¼ teaspoon crushed black pepper
- 48 parsley or cilantro leaves

PROCEDURES
Place all ingredients in a food processor or blender and process until smooth and creamy. If needed, add a touch more olive oil or water to make a firm yet creamy spread.

You can park the spread at this point up to several days in advance.

CROSTINI

INGREDIENTS

- 48 pieces of Hor D'oeurve sized bread, sliced*2
- 3 tablespoons olive oil
- 3 garlic cloves, minced
- ⅛ teaspoon crushed red pepper flakes

PROCEDURES

Toast the bread slices. You can do this by preheating an oven to 400°F. Lay the bread in a single layer on a cookie sheet and toast until golden brown (about 6-7 minutes), then turn them over, and toast for addition 3-5 minutes. You'll need to pay attention during this step as it only takes literally moments to go from beautifully toasted bread slices to awful, burned slices. Another option is to heat a cast iron grill pan and toast the bread. For added design, you can cross-hatch the bread (turn at a 90° angle for a grid grill mark rather than just straight lines), then turn over and toast the other side.

Put the olive oil, garlic, and red pepper flakes in a small frying pan and gently warm until fragrant.

This is the stage where you can park the crostini and garlic oil until assembly.

OLIVE TAPENADE

INGREDIENTS

- 2 jars pitted Kalamata Olives, drained
- 2 jars pitted green olives, drained
- ¼ cup chopped fresh parsley or cilantro
- 2 tablespoons olive oil
- 1 tablespoon balsamic vinegar
- Salt to taste*3

PROCEDURES

Using a food processor, pulse all ingredients together until you have a fine, yet still textured and chunky, tapenade.

You can park this tapenade at this point up to two days prior to assembly/serving.

*1 Use whatever herb that you used to make the tapenade.

*2 You can use Italian or French bread sliced slightly less than ¼-inch thick.

*3 I don't add salt because the olives are already brined and well-seasoned.

*4 Being of Italian descent, we call them ChiChi beans, thus, the name of this appetizer.

HERBS DE PROVENCE CASHEW CHEESE SPREAD

Serve on a platter with several different types of crackers and grapes for an appetizer that presents as beautifully as it is delicious.

INGREDIENTS

- 2 cups raw, organic cashews, soaked for 8-12 hours, then drained
- ⅜ cup nutritional yeast
- 4 garlic cloves
- 2 teaspoons sea salt
- 1 teaspoon fresh ground white pepper
- ¼-½ cup olive oil
- 1 tablespoon Herbs De Provence

PROCEDURES

Place the cashews, nutritional yeast, garlic, salt, and pepper in a food processor. Pulse several times to begin processing.

Turn on the blender and slowly drizzle in enough of the olive oil to emulsify the nut cheese while keeping it still firm.

Put the cheese into a bowl, and stir in the Herbs De Provence.

Turn the cheese into the clear glass serving vessel that you will be using to serve it in. Press the cheese down evenly and cover with parchment paper or plastic wrap firmly onto the top of the cheese. Seal the container tightly.

Cheese is best when made a week in advance and allowed to cure in the refrigerator.

Take out of the refrigerator ½-hour before serving to allow the cheese to slightly soften and the flavor to ripen.

SERVING OPTIONS

Change up the herb mixture for a different flavor profile:

For an Italian-flavored cheese, mix together basil, parsley, oregano, thyme, garlic powder, and onion powder. If you have tomato powder, that will add another dimension of earthy yet slightly sweet flavor.

For a Thai-flavored cheese, add Thai chili paste, lemon-grass, cilantro.

For an Indian-flavored cheese, add cumin, coriander, garam masala, cilantro, ginger, and garlic.

For a Moroccan-flavored cheese, add Ras el Hanout, saffron, ginger, coriander.

CHAPTER 3

SAUCES, DRESSINGS & CONDIMENTS

SAUCES, DRESSINGS, AND CONDIMENTS THAT WILL ELEVATE WHATEVER THEY ADORN.

These versatile offerings add both a flavorful and textural contrast when they are served alongside, tossed with, or adorned atop of vegetables, pastas, seitan, tofu, or crackers. They can be the difference between a great meal and a piece de résistance.

BLENDER HOLLANDAISE SAUCE

You will be absolutely amazed at the luxuriousness and silkiness of this Hollandaise Sauce. Use it to top your Eggs Benedict (using my English Muffin recipe), tofu scramble, steamed veggies, or baked potatoes.

INGREDIENTS

- ½ Haas avocado, ripe
- ½ cup plus 1 tablespoon butter
- ⅓ cup silken tofu
- 4 tablespoons filtered water
- 2 tablespoons avocado oil
- 2 tablespoons fresh-squeezed lemon juice
- 1 teaspoon yellow mustard
- ¾ teaspoon chop masala*1
- ½ teaspoon sea salt
- ½ teaspoon turmeric
- ¼ teaspoon saffron fronds
- ⅛ teaspoon cayenne, more if you want a bit of a kick (but remember, you can always add, but you can't take away)
- Black pepper to taste

PROCEDURES

Place all ingredients in a blender.

Blend until smooth.

If using a Vitamix blender or similar, continue blending until sauce is warm but not scalding, as you don't want it to break. If you do not have a Vitamix of similar blender, pour mixture in the top of a double boiler*2 and warm.

Serve immediately

***1** Chop masala is a savory Indian spice blend that can be found at all Indian grocers as well as online. Chat masala, which is another Indian spice blend will work equally well. In my opinion, other than that substitution, while you could omit this spice blend, it is really that one ingredient that makes all the difference. It will be the difference between a really flavorful and delicious Hollandaise Sauce and one that stops you in your tracks in awe.

***2** If you do not have a double boiler, put approximately 1" of water in a saucepan, and put a ceramic or stainless steel mixing bowl on top of the pot, ensuring that the bottom of the bowl fits in and covers the opening of the saucepan. Pour the sauce into the bowl and continue stirring while it warms.

Since this Hollandaise is void of eggs and butter, you do not need to worry about breaking; so you can store any leftovers in a glass container with lid. Reheat as needed, but use within 4 days or freeze.

TIP

Making a baked casserole? Toss par-boiled pasta and veggies with this Hollandaise Sauce. Pour mixture into a greased casserole pan. Sprinkle with some bread crumbs tossed with nutritional yeast, salt, pepper, and garlic powder. Bake at 365°F until it begins to bubble.

BOLOGNESE

This hearty sauce can eat like a meal just by itself; but tossed with al dente pasta, and you have one extraordinary meal. A side salad, and you are good to go. Make a double recipe and freeze the leftovers.

INGREDIENTS

- 1 large onion, small dices
- 4 tablespoons Olive Oil
- 5 carrots, peeled and chopped fine
- 8 cloves garlic
- 1 bulb fennel, including the stems, chopped*1
- 5 carrots, peeled and chopped fine
- 1 pound baby bella mushrooms*2
- 1½ pounds meatless ground beef crumble
- ½ bottle Chianti wine, or other dry red wine*3
- 1 tablespoon seasoned herbal salt
- 2 teaspoons fresh ground black pepper
- 1 teaspoon crushed red pepper flakes
- 3 28-ounce cans fire-roasted crushed tomatoes
- 1 bunch fresh basil

PROCEDURES

In a large stock pot, sauté the onions in the olive oil on medium/low heat until caramelized (but not burned), which should take approximately 20 minutes. Stir frequently.

Add the carrots, and sauté until the carrots begin to soften.

Add the garlic, and continue sautéing until the garlic is fragrant, but does not take on any color.

Add the fennel and continue sautéing until the fennel begins to slightly wilt.

Add the mushrooms, and continue sautéing until the mushrooms are cooked and most of their liquid is absorbed.

Add the meatless ground beef crumble, and sauté until heated through.

Add the wine and cook until most of the liquid is absorbed.

Add the herbal salt, black pepper, red pepper flakes, and stir to mix evenly throughout the vegetable mixture.

Add the crushed tomatoes, stirring until thoroughly combined.

Bring to a slight boil, then reduce heat to a simmer and partially cover with a lid.

Cook for 2-3 hours, stirring every 15 minutes.

Remove from heat and stir in the basil leaves.

SERVING SUGGESTION

Toss in some frozen peas when tossing with your pasta for a pop of color and an additional burst of flavor.

NOTE

You can complete this recipe up through combining all the ingredients and bringing it to a simmer, and then transfer to a crock pot to cook on medium/low for 8 hours.

*1 Don't waste the fronds. They are excellent whizzed up in a salad dressing or added to your homemade vegetable stock.

*2 You can use any variety of mushrooms that you prefer; however, try to stick with more heartier varieties.

*3 Critical rule of thumb here … if you wouldn't drink it, don't cook with it. Your final dish is only as good as the ingredients you use. And the stuff labeled "cooking wine" in the grocery stores – never allow that abomination to make its way into your shopping cart, please, I beg you.

TOMATO GRAVY

Being of Italian-American descent and a Jersey girl, we never called it 'sauce.' It's always 'gravy,' even though it's made with tomatoes and isn't brown. When I make this gravy, it's always in a huge batch so that I can freeze several containers of varying sizes. The diversity of having a homemade tomato gravy on hand is endless.

INGREDIENTS

- 1 large onion, small dices
- 4 tablespoons Olive Oil
- 8 cloves garlic, minced
- ½ bottle Chianti wine, or other dry red wine, optional but preferred[*1]
- 1 tablespoon sea salt
- 2 teaspoons fresh ground black pepper
- 2 teaspoons dried oregano or 1 tablespoon fresh
- 1 teaspoon crushed red pepper flakes
- 3 bay leaves, left whole[*2]
- 3 28-ounce cans fire-roasted crushed tomatoes
- 8-10 fresh basil leaves
- ½ cup fresh parsley, chopped

PROCEDURES

In a large stock pot, sauté the onions in the olive oil on medium/low heat until caramelized (but not burned), which should take approximately 20 minutes. Stir frequently.

Add the garlic, and continue sautéing until the garlic is fragrant, but does not take on any color.

If using the wine, add the wine and cook until most of the liquid is absorbed.

Add the salt, black pepper, oregano, red pepper flakes, and bay leaves. Stir to combine.

Add the crushed tomatoes, and stir to combine.

Bring to a slight boil, then reduce heat to a simmer and partially cover with a lid.

Cook for 2-3 hours, stirring every 15 minutes.

Remove from heat and stir in the basil and parsley.

> ***1** Critical rule of thumb here … if you wouldn't drink it, don't cook with it. Your final dish is only as good as the ingredients you use. And the stuff labeled "cooking wine" in the grocery stores – never allow that abomination to make its way into your shopping cart, please, I beg you.
>
> ***2** Remove the bay leaves prior to serving.

AUTUMN HARVEST SAUCE

A flavorful sauce celebrating the Autumnal Harvest Moon, it's wonderfully paired tossed with your favorite pasta and vegetables for a creamy primavera, used in lasagna instead of or in addition to tomato gravy, as the sauce for a baked casserole, or in a gravy boat to ladle over grilled tofu.

INGREDIENTS

- 1 small baking pumpkin*1 or 1 15-ounce can pumpkin puree
- 1 medium carrot, sliced into chunks (appx. 2 ounces)
- 1¼ cups water
- 2 teaspoons sea salt
- ½ teaspoon ground white pepper
- ¼ teaspoon rosemary
- ¼ teaspoon ground thyme or 1 teaspoon fresh thyme
- ¼ teaspoon ground cinnamon
- ¼ teaspoon ground sage or 1 teaspoon fresh sage
- ¼ teaspoon crushed red pepper flakes
- 1 pinch saffron
- ⅓ cup chopped onions
- 1 tablespoon chopped garlic (appx. 3-4 cloves)
- 1 tablespoon olive oil or butter
- ½ cup fresh pureed tomatoes (seeded)
- 1¼ cups canned coconut milk
- 1 tablespoon agave
- 2 teaspoons nutritional yeast

PROCEDURES

If you are using a fresh pumpkin, which I would highly recommend, wash the outside of the pumpkin well with warm soapy water, rinse, and dry. Preheat oven to 400°F. Cut the pumpkin in half from top to bottom. Scrape out the seeds, and set seeds aside. Place the pumpkin on a parchment paper lined cookie sheet, cut sides down. Bake for 35 minutes, or until the top of the pumpkin halves begin to cave and are soft to the touch. Allow to cool. Once cool, measure out 2 cups of pumpkin (15-16 ounces), and process in a blender until smooth. Set aside.

While the pumpkin is baking, proceed with the other steps.

Put the carrot, water, salt, pepper, rosemary, thyme, cinnamon, sage, red pepper flakes, and saffron into a small saucepan. Bring to a boil, reduce heat, and cover. Simmer until the carrot is tender and liquid is reduced in half. Set aside to cool slightly.

Sauté the onions and garlic in the olive oil or butter until translucent and tender, but do not caramelize.

Add the pureed tomatoes to the onion/garlic mixture and cook for 5 minutes. Set aside to cool slightly.

To the blender, add the pumpkin puree, carrot mixture, tomato mixture, coconut milk, agave, and nutritional yeast. Blend until combined.

*1 You can swap out the pumpkin for butternut squash or acorn squash.

PEANUT SAUCE

Perfect as a dipping sauce or a salad dressing; but I've also been known to drizzle this sauce on my breakfast fruit and yogurt for a burst of flavor. And while you can certainly use peanut butter, I prefer using the defatted powdered peanut butter for a healthy and luscious no-added-oil sauce.

INGREDIENTS
- ½ cup defatted powdered peanut butter[*1]
- ½ cup water[*1]
- ¼ cup milk[*2]
- 2 tablespoons Namu Shoyu or soy sauce
- 1 tablespoon rice vinegar
- 2 teaspoons minced fresh garlic
- 2 teaspoons agave or maple syrup
- 1 - 2 teaspoons Thai chili paste

PROCEDURES
Place all ingredients in a blender and process until smooth and creamy. Add additional milk if you would like it thinner, adding only a scant amount at a time. Remember, you can always add, but you can't take away.

[*1] If using peanut butter, omit the water.

[*2] Depending on the viscosity that you prefer, you might want to add slightly more milk. Your choice.

CASHEW CREMA

Pairs amazingly well with the Molé Black Bean Stew and Tomato Mango Lime Salsa and is equally delightful dolloped on a baked potato.

INGREDIENTS
- 2 cups cashews
- 2 tablespoons lime juice, separated
- 5 cups water, separated
- ½ cup cilantro, stems and leaves
- ½ jalapeno, seeded (optional)
- 1¼ teaspoons salt
- ½ teaspoon white ground pepper

PROCEDURES
Soak the cashews and 1 tablespoon lime juice with 4 cups of water overnight.

Drain and rinse cashews.

In blender, add the cashews, the remaining 1 tablespoon lime juice, 1 cup water, salt, and pepper; and blend until smooth.

For ease in serving and presentation purposes, pour into squeeze bottles.

ROASTED RED PEPPER CHIMICHURRI

A riff on the Classic Chimichurri[*1], the slightly-sweet, charred flavor of the roasted peppers adds another dimension to this herbaceous sauce.

INGREDIENTS
- 1 16-ounce jar of roasted red peppers, drained
- 1¼ cups parsley
- ¾ cup cilantro
- ½ cup extra virgin olive oil
- ⅓ cup red wine vinegar (or 2 tablespoons balsamic vinegar with apple cider vinegar to make ⅓ cup)
- 3 garlic cloves
- 1 shallot
- ¾ teaspoon crushed red pepper flakes
- ½ teaspoon cumin
- ½ teaspoon sea salt

PROCEDURES
Process all ingredients in a blender just until combined but with a copious amount of texture remaining.

[*1] To make a classic chimichurri, swap out the peppers for additional parsley and cilantro.

TOMATO MANGO LIME SALSA

The salsa is ideal as the condiment to the Molé Black Bean Stew coupled with the Cashew Lime Crema. You'll also enjoy it scooped up with tortilla chips or as the crowning glory to a burrito.

INGREDIENTS
- 12 Roma tomatoes
- 4 mangoes
- 1 medium red onion
- 1 jalapeno
- ½ cup Cilantro leaves*1
- Juice and zest from 3 limes
- 2 teaspoons Salt
- 1 teaspoon black pepper

PROCEDURES
Seed and chop the tomatoes into small chunks. Park in a large mixing bowl.

Dice the mangoes into dices of equal size to the tomatoes and add to the bowl.

Chop the onion into very small dices. Add to bowl.

*1 Use the cilantro stems to make Cilantro Chutney.

Mince jalapeno and add to bowl.

Chop cilantro and add to bowl.

Add lime juice, salt and pepper.

Stir to combine.

Park in refrigerator to chill.

PARSLEY CASHEW DIPPING SAUCE

This is the perfect dipping sauce to serve alongside the Winter Rolls.

INGREDIENTS
- 1 bunch of parsley
- ⅓ cup cashew butter
- Juice and zest from 2 lemons
- 2-3 garlic cloves
- 1 teaspoon sea salt
- ½ teaspoon crushed black pepper
- Pinch of red pepper flakes or hot sauce

PROCEDURES
Put all the ingredients in a blender and process until smooth.

If the dipping sauce is too thick, you can add a scant amount of lemon juice or water to reach the desired consistency.

OPTIONS
Swap out parsley for another herb and/or the cashew butter for a different nut butter — such as, macadamia nut butter.

SWEET & SOUR DIPPING SAUCE

This sauce is perfect served as a condiment to any Oriental appetizer or main dish.

INGREDIENTS
- 3½ tablespoons corn starch
- 1 cup water, separated
- ¾ cup unrefined cane sugar
- ⅓ cup ketchup
- 1 tablespoon tamari
- ¼ teaspoon sea salt
- ½ cup vinegar

PROCEDURES
In a small bowl, whisk together the corn starch and ⅓ cup water. Set aside.

In a saucepan, combine the sugar, ⅔ cup water, ketchup, tamari, and salt. Cook over medium high heat, stirring frequently for five minutes.

Add the vinegar, and stir to combine.

Add the corn starch slurry to the pot, and cook, stirring constantly, until mixture thickens (allow to come to gentle boil, then reduce heat to a simmer, stirring constantly for an additional minute).

Set aside to cool before serving.

INDIAN CILANTRO CHUTNEY

One of my favorite condiments, I put this chutney on pretty much anything that is savory, it doesn't have to be Indian. Add a touch of olive oil, and you have the perfect salad dressing.

INGREDIENTS
- 1 bunch cilantro, including stems
- Juice and zest of two lemons
- 3 cloves garlic
- ½ jalapeno, optional, but recommended
- 2 teaspoons sea salt

PROCEDURES
Process all ingredients in a blender just until combined. You can leave some texture or process until smooth.

HORSERADISH SAUCE

Fresh-shredded horseradish, accompanied by the cilantro, elevates horseradish sauce to new heights. Serve this with the Chesapeake Bay Crabby Cakes for an ethereal trip to the Baltimore Harbor.

INGREDIENTS
- 1½ cups mayonnaise
- 8 ounce container cream cheese
- 1 cup yogurt
- 1 tablespoon powdered mustard
- Salt and pepper to taste
- 1½ cups fresh shredded horseradish
- ½ cup cilantro

PROCEDURES
In a mixing bowl, whisk together the mayonnaise, cream cheese, and yogurt until well combined and smooth.

Whisk in powdered mustard, salt, and pepper.

Stir in horseradish and cilantro.

LEMON-CHIVE DRESSING

This citrus-forward dressing works equally well as a salad dressing as it does a marinade.

INGREDIENTS
- 2 tablespoons Olive Oil
- 2 tablespoons fresh-squeeze lemon juice and zest from the lemon
- 2 tablespoons White Balsamic Vinegar[*1]
- 2 teaspoons agave
- 2 tablespoons minced chives
- Sea salt and freshly-ground pepper to taste

PROCEDURES
Whisk all the ingredients together in a small bowl. Set aside.

[*1] If you don't have White Balsamic Vinegar available, you can use Rice Wine Vinegar or Apple Cider Vinegar.

MAPLE HARISSA DRESSING

Harissa is what thrusts what would otherwise be an ordinary vinaigrette into a flavor sensation that can easily hold up, yet not overpower, roasted vegetables.

INGREDIENTS
- ½ cup olive oil
- ⅓ cup Balsamic Vinegar
- 3 tablespoons maple syrup
- 2 teaspoons Harissa
- ¼ teaspoon sea salt
- 2 teaspoons flat-leave parsley
- 1 teaspoon fresh thyme

PROCEDURES
Place the oil, balsamic vinegar, maple syrup, Harissa, and salt in a blender. Process until smooth.

Transfer to a bowl and whisk in the parsley and thyme.

Set aside.

Refrigerate if not using immediately.

CHAPTER 4

SOUPS

EASY BREEZY SATISFYING SOUPS THAT CAN BE WHIPPED UP IN A JIFFY.

With a well-stocked pantry, you can prepare these comforting, ambrosial soups quickly and easily. Some of the recipes taste like they took all day; yet you don't even have to cook them if you choose to not do so. Served either at room temperature, cold, or warmed, they are substantial and flavorful. And then we have also included those soups that simmer on the stovetop, their aroma permeating throughout the kitchen, bringing comfort and warmth to ward off the chill in the air.

GAZPACHO

A perfectly refreshing cold soup from the summer garden bounty of tomatoes, this soup can be made equally fabulous using beautifully ripe organic Roma tomatoes purchased from your grocer.

INGREDIENTS

- 3 pounds ripe Roma tomatoes, peeled, cored, seeded, and coarsely chopped*1
- 1 seedless cucumber, peeled and coarsely chopped
- 2 red bell peppers, seeded and coarsely chopped
- 1 jalapeno, coarsely chopped (seeded if you do not want the extra heat)
- ⅓ cup olive oil
- ¼ cup Aged Balsamic Vinegar, or White Balsamic Vinegar
- Sea salt and freshly-ground black pepper to taste
- Optional: Chopped herbs, Arugula and/or pepitas.

PROCEDURES

For the optimal flavor profile, toss together the tomatoes, cucumber, peppers, jalapeno, oil, and vinegar in a large mixing bowl and park in the refrigerator for 12-24 hours before processing. If time is of the essence, however, just go for it.

In a blender, puree all ingredients, except salt and pepper, until smooth and silky.

Season to taste with sea salt and black pepper.

Serve in soup bowls.

You can garnish with arugula, chopped cilantro, parsley, and/or roughly chopped pepitas.

*1 For a fire-roasted flavor, roast or grill the tomatoes until the skin is charred before peeling. Although I don't typically recommend using canned tomatoes for this recipe as they oftentimes tend to leave a sort of tin-like aftertaste if they are not cooked; you could also use an extremely high-grade organic canned tomato for a decent and quick variation; but you will lose the freshness.

TIP

Leftovers? Toss the soup into cooked rice and gently warm through for a lovely side dish. Make it a hearty one-dish meal by also adding in whatever cooked or canned beans you have on hand.

CREAMY-DREAMY CANNELLINI BEAN SOUP

This is a robust soup that you can enjoy whether you opt for cold, room temperature, or hot. If you are going to serve this soup warmed through, I recommend using a double boiler to avoid the bottom of your soup scorching, or heat using a very low flame, stirring frequently.

INGREDIENTS
- 2 (15 oz) cans cannellini beans, drained[*1]
- 2 cups unchicken broth, separated
- 1 leek, rinsed well and chopped
- 1 shallot, chopped
- 3 garlic cloves, chopped
- 1 stick celery, chopped and deveined
- 1 tablespoon extra-virgin olive oil
- 1 teaspoon dry oregano, or 1 tablespoon fresh oregano
- 1 teaspoon sea salt
- ¼ teaspoon freshly ground black pepper
- ¼-½ teaspoon crushed red pepper flakes, optional

PROCEDURES

Combine all ingredients in a blender, reserving 1 cup of the unchicken broth. Process until smooth and creamy.

Add additional unchicken broth to reach your desired consistency.

Season with additional sea salt and black pepper to taste, as necessary.

Serve in soup bowls.

OPTIONAL GARNISH
Top with a drizzle of Olive Oil and chopped herbs.

[*1] Have a hankering for a potato soup? Swap out the cannellini beans with an equal amount of boiled potatoes, and you have the wonderful riff on the classic cold potato soup, Vichyssoise. Served warm, this option is equally delightful. Have leftover mashed potatoes? You can use them as well; although I recommend starting out with ½ cup unchicken broth and slowly adding in the broth until you reach your desired consistency. Remember, you can always add, but you can't take away.

TIP
Are you looking for a bean soup with texture rather than a pureed, creamy soup? Easy enough using this recipe. Start by sautéing the leeks, shallot, and garlic cloves in the olive oil until fragrant, but don't allow them to take on any color. Add the broth and simmer for 5-10 minutes before adding in the beans, oregano, salt, pepper and red pepper flakes. Simmer an additional 15 minutes. Serve warm/hot.

MINESTRA DI VERDURA E RISO

Italian Vegetable & Rice Soup: Make a double batch of brown rice one evening, and you have a quick and easy dinner for the following night.

INGREDIENTS
- 3 cups frozen broccoli, defrosted
- 2 cups cooked brown rice
- 1½ to 2 cups unchicken broth
- 1 cup fresh basil, chopped, separated
- ¼ cup extra-virgin Olive Oil
- 2 shallots, roughly chopped
- 3-4 cloves garlic, chopped
- 1½ teaspoons sea salt
- ½ teaspoon freshly-ground black pepper

PROCEDURES

FOR PUREED BLENDER SOUP
Put the rice, broccoli, 1½ cups unchicken broth, ½ cup basil, olive oil, shallots, garlic, salt, and pepper in blender. Process until combined leaving some texture.

Add additional unchicken broth for desired consistency.

Serve in soup bowls. Garnish with remaining ½ cup basil.

FOR A CHUNKY SOUP
SERVED EITHER HOT OR COLD
Lightly sautè the shallots and garlic in the olive oil until fragrant, about 1 - 2 minutes.

Add the broth and bring to a boil. Simmer 10 minutes.

Add the rice and broccoli.

Bring to a boil, and reduce to simmer for 15 minutes.

Remove from heat and stir in half the basil, along with the salt and pepper.

Serve in bowls. Garnish with remaining chopped basil.

THAI CORN COCONUT SOUP

This soup is a complete homage to the bounty of fresh-picked corn. Every summer, I look forward to the announcement that the local corn farm is open for business. You have to be there by 9-10am, otherwise you'll be out of luck for that day. The bright, crisp freshness of the just-harvested corn is what truly makes this soup one to remember. It has become my go-to summer soup. Ah, but not to be deterred. When fresh-picked corn is not available, you can use organic frozen corn with very respectable results.

INGREDIENTS

- 2 cups corn (about 4 ears fresh corn, or 2 cups frozen and thawed)
- 1 13.5-ounce can coconut milk (full fat)
- 2 tablespoons fresh-squeeze lime juice
- 3 kaffir lime leaves, chopped (or 1 tablespoon lime zest)
- 1 shallot, chopped
- 3 cloves garlic, chopped
- 1" piece of fresh galangal, finely minced (or 2 teaspoons dry)
- 1" piece of fresh ginger, finely minced (or 2 teaspoons dry)
- 1 teaspoon unrefined dark brown sugar or 1 teaspoon brown rice syrup
- 1 teaspoon ground cumin
- ¾ teaspoon ground coriander
- ½ teaspoon turmeric
- ¼-½ teaspoon dried crushed chili, or ½ teaspoons chili sauce
- Chopped fresh cilantro for garnish

PROCEDURES

Place all ingredients, except the cilantro, into blender and process until well combined. You can process this soup leaving some texture (my personal favorite) or take it to a creamy, smooth soup, your choice.

Garnish with fresh chopped cilantro

OPTIONS

This soup works as an amazing 'sauce' for a casserole. Toss it into sliced potatoes with some nutritional yeast for a scalloped potato casserole. Mix it with a blend of blanched vegetables and bake; and you have yourself a mighty delicious vegetable casserole. And of course, we couldn't mention baked casseroles without mentioning a pasta casserole. Mix it up. Honest, you will be positively enchanted with the results that come out of your oven.

CAULIFLOWER & MACARONI SOUP

This soup is a riff on my Grandma Mary's Broccoli and Macaroni Soup. Growing up, whenever Grandma Mary asked what I wanted to eat for lunch, my answer was unanimously always the same response, "Broccoli and Macaroni Soup". I thought it was a masterpiece, so quick and simple. It was probably one of the first, if not the first, recipes she taught me how to cook.

Her version consisted of opening up a bag of frozen broccoli into a stock pot, covering the broccoli completely with water, bringing it up to a boil, then adding in some elbow macaroni. She'd cook it until the pasta was al dente, then serve it in soup bowls, drizzling a touch of olive oil over the steaming soup. Heaven, pure heaven to that little girl who was, by the time the soup was served, drooling with anticipation.

Now, I have to admit, that I still, to this day, am known to whip up that bowlful of memories. However, I have also taken some adult creative license to that joyous bowl filled with love. And I am sharing that with you now.

INGREDIENTS

- 1 head of cauliflower, cut into bite sized pieces
- Water to cover
- 2 teaspoons sea salt
- ¾ pound ditali pasta (or ditallini or elbow pasta)
- 4 garlic cloves, minced
- 1 tablespoon olive oil
- 1 teaspoon red pepper flakes
- Sea salt and fresh ground black pepper to taste

PROCEDURES

While the soup is cooking, in a small pan, gently simmer the garlic in the olive oil until perfumed but not colored. Remove from heat and stir in the red pepper flakes. Set aside.

Place the cauliflower in a stock pot.

Add water to cover plus an additional ½" high.

Bring to a boil, then add the 2 teaspoons sea salt.

Reduce to a simmer, simmering for 20-25 minutes, or until the cauliflower is tender and the aroma of cauliflower is permeating your kitchen.

Add the pasta, and simmer for two minutes less than the suggested cook time on the bag/box of pasta.

Remove from heat, stir in the garlic oil.

Season to taste with salt and pepper

SERVING SUGGESTION

Serve with grated Parmesan cheese or a mixture of toasted nuts, nutritional yeast, and sea salt that has been processed to mimic a grated cheese. You can also serve with fresh-chopped parsley.

BLACK BEAN SOUP

Cooked in an InstantPot, this one-pot soup is not only effortless and time-efficient but also an earthy, stick-to-your-ribs satisfying soup that eats as a main dish.

INGREDIENTS

- 1½ cups dry black beans, quick soaked[*1] or soaked overnight, drained and rinsed
- 2 tablespoons Olive Oil
- 1 large onion, chopped
- 4-5 garlic cloves, minced
- 1 tablespoon ground cumin
- 1 teaspoon chipotle powder[*2]
- 6 cups unchicken broth
- 2 bay leafs
- 2 teaspoons oregano, dry; or 4 teaspoons, fresh
- 2 teaspoons sea salt
- 1 teaspoon freshly ground black pepper
- 1 cup cilantro, chopped
- Sour cream, optional
- Salsa, optional
- Avocado, optional

PROCEDURES

In the InstantPot, sauté the onion in the oil for two minutes.

Add the garlic, cumin, and chipotle powder, and sauté for an additional one minute.

Add the beans, broth, bay leaf, oregano, sea salt, and black pepper.

Lock the lid of the InstantPot in place.

Turn the steam valve to "sealed".

Click the "soup" button.

Set time to 30 minutes.

When it beeps that it's done, allow pressure to come down naturally.

Carefully remove lid.

Remove bay leaf, and mash some of the black beans manually or with an immersion blender to make a thicker soup.

Garnish with cilantro, vegan sour cream, Avocado and/or salsa.

[*1] **How to Quick-Soak Beans:** Forgot to soak your beans overnight? If so, no worries. Rinse the beans well, then place in a stock pot and cover with water 1" above the beans. Bring to a boil and boil for one minute. Remove from heat, cover, and set aside for one hour. Do not open the lid during this time as you want to keep all the heat inside the pot. Drain and rinse.

[*2] You can use a dry chipotle chili if you don't have chipotle powder. Seed it, then grind in a spice grinder. If you don't have either, you can certainly swap it out for chili powder.

BUTTERNUT SQUASH SOUP WITH ALMOND CREAM & SPICED PUMPKIN SEEDS

A truly substantial soup that needs nothing more than maybe a crusty slice of sourdough bread to sop up the remains of the soup at the bottom of the bowl, ensuring that nothing is left behind.

INGREDIENTS

- 1 cup diced white onion
- 1 cup chopped apple
- ¼ cup olive oil
- ½ teaspoon cinnamon
- ½ teaspoon chopped fresh sage
- ½ teaspoon chopped fresh rosemary
- ½ lemongrass stalk, split (or 1 teaspoon ground lemongrass)
- ½ chipotle chili in adobo sauce
- 1½ teaspoons sea salt
- 3 pounds butternut squash, peeled, seeded, and chopped
- 8 cups vegetable stock
- 1 recipe Almond Cream (recipe follows below)
- 1 recipe Spiced Pumpkin Seeds (recipe below)

PROCEDURES

Sauté the onions and apples in the olive oil in a large heavy soup pot over medium/low heat, stirring occasionally, for 8-10 minutes, until the onions and apples become translucent without caramelizing.

Add the cinnamon, sage, rosemary, lemongrass, chipotle chili, and salt. Continue to sauté for another 3-4 minutes, to bring out the fragrance of the herbs and spices.

Add the butternut squash and stir to coat.

Add the stock, bring to a boil, and decrease the heat to simmer.

Cook, covered, until the squash is tender, about 40 minutes.

If you used fresh lemongrass, remove the stalk.

Let soup cool enough to process in a blender, or use an immersion blender until smooth.

Serve with a dollop of the Almond Cream and a sprinkling of the Pumpkin Seeds.

ALMOND CREAM

INGREDIENTS

- 2 cups sliced, peeled almonds
- 3 tablespoons olive oil
- 2 tablespoons fresh-squeezed lemon juice
- ½ cup water
- 1 tablespoon fresh chives, chopped

PROCEDURES

Soak the almonds in enough water to cover them for at least 8-12 hours in the refrigerator.

Drain and rinse the nuts, then transfer to a blender.

Add the oil, lemon juice and water. Blend until smooth.

Stir in the chives.

Transfer to a covered bowl and refrigerate until ready to use.

SPICED PUMPKIN SEEDS

INGREDIENTS

- 1 cup pumpkin seeds, hulled
- 1 tablespoon olive oil
- 1½ teaspoons fresh lemon juice
- Pinch of garlic powder, ground cinnamon, sea salt, and ground black pepper

PROCEDURES

Preheat oven to 300°F with cookie sheet in oven.

Combine and toss all the ingredients in a bowl until thoroughly coated.

Carefully remove cookie sheet, spread pumpkin seed mixture evenly in pan, and return pan to oven.

Roast for 5 to 10 minutes, shaking the pan occasionally to avoid burning, until the seeds are lightly browned. Watch this step carefully and closely. It's only a matter of seconds between perfectly-roasted seeds and burned to lack of recognition.

Remove from oven, and transfer to uncovered bowl to cool.

ROASTED CELERY, LEEK AND POTATO SOUP WITH BACON AND GREMOLATA GARNISH

INGREDIENTS

- 1 head (approximately 3 cups) celery hearts, peeled and chopped, reserving the celery leaves and baby stalks
- 2 medium leeks, washed and sliced
- 6 cloves of garlic, peeled
- 2 tablespoons olive oil, separated
- 1 tablespoon raw coconut vinegar
- 1 teaspoon celery seeds
- 1 teaspoon sea salt
- ½ teaspoon white pepper
- 4-5 cups unchicken broth, separated
- 2-3 medium Yukon gold potatoes, cubed
- ⅓ cup creamer, unsweetened (optional, but definitely recommended)
- 4 ounces seitan, sliced very thin and chopped to resemble bacon crumbles
- 1 teaspoon liquid smoke
- 1 recipe Gremolata (Recipe below)

PROCEDURES

Preheat oven to 400°F with a rimmed cookie sheet in the oven.

In a large bowl, toss together the celery hearts, leeks, garlic, olive oil reserving a scant amount for later, vinegar, celery seeds, sea salt, and pepper.

Carefully remove the baking sheet from the oven, and spread the vegetable mixture evenly in the pan.

Return the baking sheet to the oven; and roast vegetables until they are caramelized in spots, approximately 30-35 minutes.

While roasting the vegetables, cook the potatoes in 2 cups of the chicken broth. When the potatoes are cooked through, puree the potatoes and their cooking liquid with the 2 additional cups of broth and set aside.

While roasting the vegetables, toss the seiten in the liquid smoke, then brown/crisp the seitan in the remaining scant amount of oil. Drain and set aside.

When the vegetables are roasted, remove from oven.

Working in batches, puree the vegetables with the potato puree until smooth.

Transfer the pureed soup into a soup pot. If the soup is too thick, use the remaining one cup of broth to thin the soup.

When all the soup and broth has been combined and pureed, gently warm the soup, adding the creamer.

To serve, ladle the soup into a soup bowl. Garnish with the celery gremolata and bacon bits.

GREMOLATA*1

INGREDIENTS

- Reserved celery leaves and baby stalks
- 1 cup fresh parsley
- 2-3 garlic cloves
- Zest and juice from 1 lemon
- Salt and pepper

PROCEDURES

In a food processor or blender, combine all ingredients until blended into a chunky puree. You want this condiment to have texture but not large bits.

*1 A Gremolata is typically made with only parsley; however, since this is a celery-forward soup, I thought it only fitting to carry the theme throughout and into the Gremolata.

CHAPTER 5
SALADS

ROBUST, FLAVORFUL, AND COLORFUL, THESE ARE SALADS THAT CAN EAT LIKE A MEAL OR BE A BOLD ACCOMPANIMENT IN A MEAL.

Tired of the same run-of-the-mill nightly side salad? Too hot to heat up the kitchen but looking for something light and refreshing yet hearty? Do you have a craving for a colorful, mouthwatering salad for your entree? If so, we have your answers in this chapter.

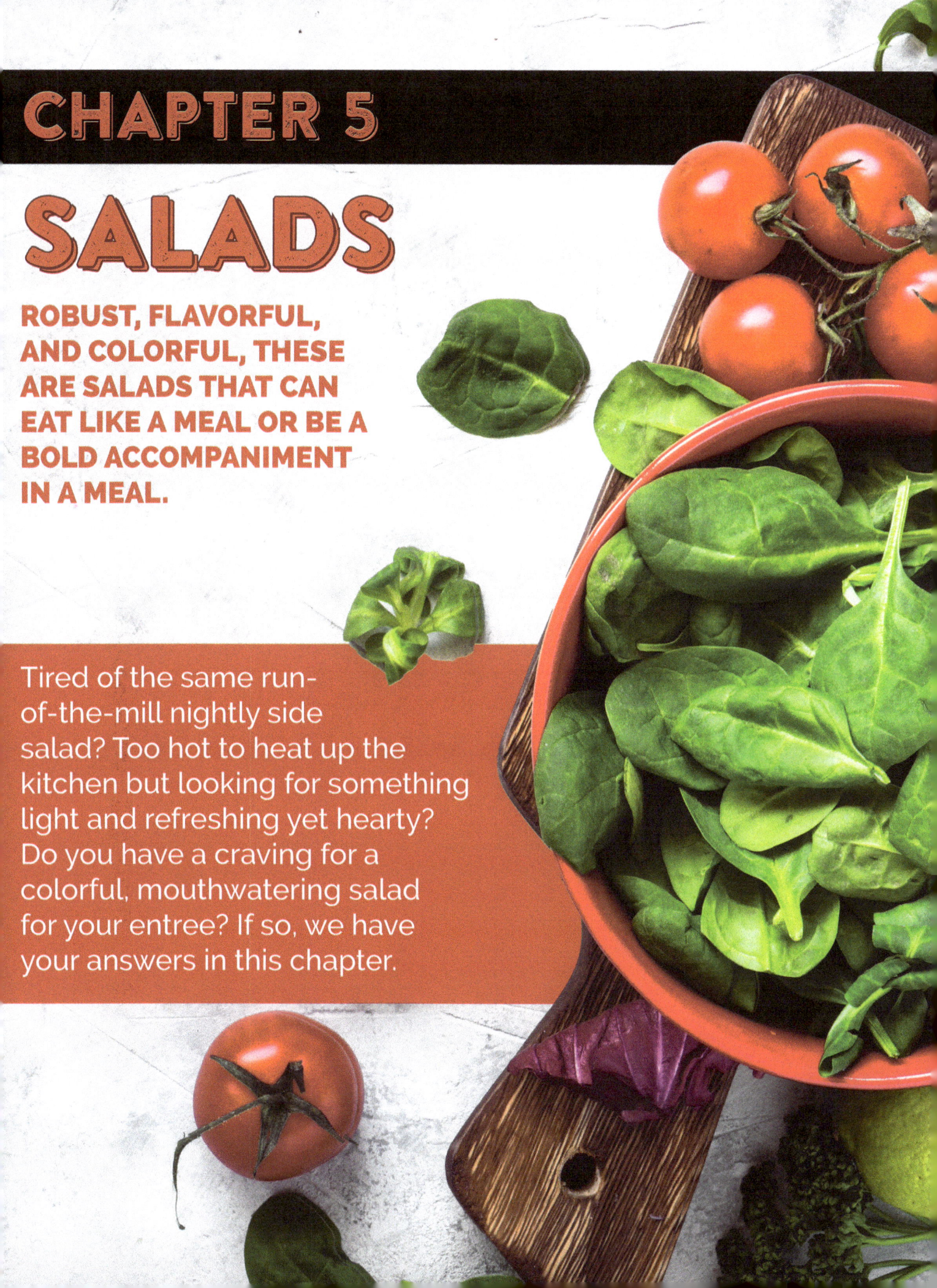

APPLE FENNEL SALAD

This refreshing salad combines both fruit and veggies for that sweet yet savory taste sensation. It can easily stand on its own but would also be a wonderful accompaniment to grilled tofu or tempeh.

INGREDIENTS

- 1 blood orange, juice and zest
- 2 tablespoons olive oil
- 1 tablespoon fresh flat-leaf parsley or mint, chopped
- 1 teaspoon anise seeds, slightly crushed in mortar/pestle
- Sea salt & freshly ground black pepper to taste
- 1 Fuji apple, diced
- 1 Granny Smith apple diced
- 1 medium fennel bulb, sliced in thin strips
- ¼ small red onion, sliced in thin strips
- 1 small bunch arugula, broken

PROCEDURES

Prepare the dressing by combining the orange juice and zest, olive oil, parsley (or mint), anise seeds, sea salt, and black pepper. You can use a whisk or blender for this step. If using a blender, do not add the zest, anise seeds, and parsley/mint to the blender. Stir/whisk them in after combining the other ingredients. Set aside.

In a large mixing bowl, toss together the apples, fennel, and onion.

Pour in the dressing, and toss to coat.

Arrange the arugula on a platter, then nestle the salad on top of the arugula, leaving a border of the greens as an accent.

OPTION

You can either toss the arugula into the salad or serve the salad nested on a bed of arugula.

GRILLED CAESAR SALAD WITH BUTTERMILK DILL DRESSING AND FOCACCIA CRUMBLE

Yes, grilled romaine lettuce. The slight char to the greens adds a whole new dimension of complexity to this simple, yet elegant, salad.

INGREDIENTS

- 1 recipe Buttermilk Ranch dill dressing (recipe on opposite page)
- 4 slices of leftover Focaccia (recipe can be found in the Yeast Doughs section)
- 1 - 2 heads Romaine Lettuce hearts
- Olive oil in spritzer
- Fleur de Sel Salt
- Fresh ground black pepper

PROCEDURES

Prepare the dressing. Park in the refrigerator until ready to use.

Break up focaccia into large chunks and put into food processor. Using the pulse option, pulse the cubes until broken down but still have quite a bit of texture remaining. If desired, toss them with a teaspoon of nutritional yeast, ¼ teaspoon of oregano, some fresh ground black pepper.

Set aside.

Preheat grill or grill pan to screaming hot.

Cut romaine hearts in half lengthwise. Depending on how large they are, you can quarter them, but they will hold together better and present more attractively when cut in half. Do not cut out the core.

PROCEDURES CONT.

Lightly spritz the flat cut side with olive oil.

Place the lettuce cut side down on the grill. Do not move about. Allow it to grill until you can easily remove it, and there are grill marks. You will be able to tell because the side of the lettuce will begin to gently wilt. Do not over-grill. We are not looking for cooked lettuce, just slightly charred.

Remove from the grill and place on a platter grilled side up.

Season lightly with salt and pepper.

Drizzle the ranch dressing on top.

Sprinkle the focaccia crumbles over lettuce and dressing.

Serve immediately.

BUTTERMILK RANCH DRESSING

INGREDIENTS

- ¾ cup cashews
- 2 tablespoons lemon juice, separated
- ½ cup soy milk
- 1 teaspoon dried dill or 2 teaspoons fresh dill
- 1 teaspoon salt
- ½ teaspoon dried parsley, or 1 teaspoon fresh parsley
- ½ teaspoon dried chives, or 1 teaspoon fresh chives
- ½ teaspoon garlic powder, or ¾ teaspoon fresh minced garlic
- ¼ teaspoon onion powder
- ¼ teaspoon fresh ground white pepper

PROCEDURES

Soak the cashews overnight with 1 tablespoon lemon juice and enough water to cover plus 2".

Whisk the remaining lemon juice with the soy milk, and allow it sit for 10 minutes. Set aside.

Drain and rinse the cashews.

In a high-powered blender, add the cashews and soy milk. Blend until smooth. If the dressing is too thick, add a scant amount of water to attain the desired viscosity.

Add the dill, salt, parsley, chives, garlic powder, onion powder, salt, and pepper; and pulse to combine.

Taste, and adjust seasoning, if desired.

For ease in serving and presentation purposes, pour into squeeze bottles.

MIDDLE EASTERN FARRO SALAD

Farro, a grain that is indigenous to the Fertile Crescent, otherwise referred to as the "Cradle of Civilization," it is familiarly used in cuisine from the Tuscany region of Italy. A frequent use is in soups or as risotto. It is a hearty, whole grain in the wheat family. When you chew, it has a sort of 'pop' one would associate with wheat berries. It has a nutty flavor and makes for a robust, unique salad.

INGREDIENTS

- 1½ cups whole-grain farro
- Water to cover
- 2½ cups unchicken broth
- ¼ cup plus a splash White Balsamic Vinegar*1, separated
- 1 cup thinly sliced cucumber
- ½ cup sliced Kalamata olives, drained, reserving 1 tablespoon brine for the dressing
- 2 avocados
- Pinch of salt
- 5 cups baby spinach leaves, broken
- 1 Recipe Lemon-Chive Dressing
- 1 batch Crumbled Za'atar Tofu (recipe to the right)

PROCEDURES

Place farro in a bowl and cover with cool water. Cover bowl and allow farro to soak 8-16 hours.*2

To prepare the farro for cooking, drain and rinse.

In a medium-sized saucepan, add the farro, unchicken broth, and ¼ cup vinegar. Bring to a boil, then reduce to a gentle simmer, cover and cook until done but still toothsome (approximately 15 minutes).

When done, drain the farro and place it in a large mixing bowl. Using a fork, fluff the farro to separate the kernels and cool the farro. Be careful not to break the farro.

Add the cucumbers and the Kalamata olives to the farro. Gently toss to combine.

Prepare the avocados. Cut open the avocados and remove the stone. Using a paring knife (and being careful to not cut through the skin), slice into the avocado flesh to create small cubes. Using a tablespoon, run the spoon between the skin and the flesh to remove the cubes. In a small mixing bowl, gently toss the avocados with the remaining splash of vinegar, adding a pinch of salt. Add to the farro mixture.

Add the spinach to the farro mixture.

Add the dressing, and gently toss to combine.

Top with the Crumbled Za'atar Tofu

CRUMBLED ZA'ATAR TOFU
INGREDIENTS

- 8 ounces extra-firm sprouted tofu
- 1 tablespoon za'atar seasoning (recipe below)
- 1 tablespoon Kalamata olive brine
- 1 tablespoon lemon juice
- ½ tablespoon olive oil

PROCEDURES

Using a tofu press or clean, dry towel, press tofu to remove moisture.

Crumble tofu into a mixing bowl.

In a separate small bowl, whisk together the za'atar, olive brine, lemon juice, and olive oil.

Pour the dressing over the tofu and toss to coat.

Refrigerate until ready to use. This crumble is best when it is prepared at least several hours in advance to allow the flavors to marinate throughout the tofu.

ZA'ATAR SEASONING
INGREDIENTS

- 1 tablespoon sumac berries or powder
- 1 tablespoon sesame seeds
- 1½ teaspoons dried oregano
- 1½ teaspoons dried thyme
- 2 teaspoons sea salt

PROCEDURES

Combine all ingredients together using a spice or coffee grinder by quickly pulsing 2-3 times. Do not over-process as you would like some texture rather than a powder.

*1 If you don't have White Balsamic Vinegar on hand, a rice vinegar or cider vinegar would be just fine as a swap-out.

*2 No worries if you didn't soak the farro. It will just take longer to cook, approximately 30 minutes.

ROASTED BRUSSELS SPROUTS, APPLES, CRANBERRIES AND WALNUT SALAD

Tossed with the Maple-Harissa Dressing, you will be transported immediately to the North African Country of Tunisia

INGREDIENTS

- 3 pounds Brussels sprouts, trimmed and halved
- 2 tablespoons olive oil
- 4 garlic cloves, minced
- ½ teaspoon fresh rosemary, chopped
- ½ teaspoon sea salt
- ¼ teaspoon freshly ground black pepper
- 4 shallots, sliced
- 2 red apples, cored and thinly sliced tossed in 1 teaspoon lemon juice to retard oxidation
- 1 cup dried cranberries
- 1 cup chopped roasted walnuts
- 1 Recipe of Maple-Harissa Dressing

PROCEDURES

Preheat oven to 365°F with a large cookie sheet in the oven.

In a large bowl, toss the Brussels sprouts with the olive oil, garlic, rosemary, salt, and black pepper, coating evenly.

Carefully remove cookie sheet from oven. Working quickly and being careful because the cookie sheet will be hot, evenly spread the Brussels sprouts on the cookie sheet, then return to oven.

Roast for 20 minutes.

Remove from oven, and sprinkle the shallots over the Brussels sprouts. Return the pan into the oven, and roast for an additional 15 minutes.

Remove from oven, transfer the Brussels Sprouts to a bowl, and allow them to cool.

Combine the Brussels sprouts with the apples, cranberries, and walnuts.

Add the Maple-Harissa Dressing and toss until coated.

Serve immediately, or refrigerate.

CREAMY PASTA PRIMAVERA SALAD

Either as a side or main dish, this pasta salad is a jaw-dropping delight. Perfect for that summer barbeque yet nourishingly substantial enough for a cold winter's night entrée.

INGREDIENTS

- ⅔ cup dried cannellini beans (or 2 cups canned, drained)
- Water to cover beans (omit if using canned)
- 8 garlic cloves (if dried beans), separated or 1½ teaspoons garlic powder (if canned beans)
- 3 small zucchinis, halved lengthwise and sliced ¼" thick
- 2 small yellow squash, halved lengthwise and sliced ¼" thick
- 3 red bell peppers, roasted, peeled, and sliced (or 1 cup jarred roasted red peppers, drained and sliced)
- 2 cups broccoli florets, blanched until just al dente and cut into small bite-size florets
- 1½ cups frozen peas, thawed
- 1½ cups carrots, sliced wafer-thin or julienned
- 1 cup fresh flat-leaf parsley, chopped
- 1 cup fresh basil, chopped
- 1 pound penne rigate pasta
- ¾ cup plus 1 tablespoon olive oil, separated
- Juice and zest from 1 lemon
- 1 cup cashews, soaked for 2-3 hours
- ⅓ cup nutritional yeast
- ⅓ cup White balsamic vinegar*1
- 1 tablespoon fresh oregano (or 1½ teaspoons dried)
- 1 tablespoon fresh thyme (or 1½ teaspoons dried)
- 1 teaspoon fresh rosemary
- Sea salt and freshly-ground black pepper to taste
- Water to thin, if necessary

PROCEDURES

If using dry beans, soak beans 4-8 hours in water that is 2" above the beans. Add 3 slightly-crushed garlic cloves, bring to a boil, lower to a simmer, cover, and cook for approximately 30-40 minutes, until beans are tender but not mushy. You want them to hold their shape in the salad. If the beans did not soak, allow 50-60 minutes for beans to cook. Drain and set aside in large mixing bowl.

If using canned beans, drain beans, very lightly rinse to remove the starchy water, and toss with garlic powder. Set aside in large mixing bowl.

In a large sauté pan on medium-high heat, sauté the zucchini and yellow squash in a scant amount of olive oil until slightly brown and gently cooked through, but still toothsome. Add to bowl.

Roast the red bell peppers over an open flame on your gas burner or grill, grill pan, or in a pre-heated 450°F oven until charred all around. Put in a clean brown paper bag and seal closed or in a glass bowl covered with plastic wrap. Allow peppers to sweat and cool. When cooled, peel skins, remove seeds, and slice. Never run roasted peppers under water as that will also remove much of their flavor. Add to bowl.

Add broccoli florets, peas, carrots, parsley, and basil to the bowl. Gently toss to combine.

Cook pasta in salted water until al dente (Using package instructions, start testing 3 minutes before cooking time directions.) Drain and rinse under cool water to stop cooking process. Toss with 1 tablespoon olive oil and lemon juice, then add the pasta to the beans and vegetables.

In a blender, combine the remaining olive oil, remaining lemon juice, lemon zest, cashews, sea salt and black pepper. Add a touch of water or lemon juice if it needs thinning.

Pour dressing into pasta/veggies, and gently toss to combine.

Best when allowed to marinate in the refrigerator for 4 hours before serving.

OPTIONS

Make it your own by swapping out some of the vegetables for other varieties.

While this recipe is written to be served as a cold salad, it is equally delicious served at room temperature or even baked as a casserole in the oven until warmed through. If you are going to bake it as a casserole, sprinkle bread crumbs over the top before baking.

*1 If you don't have access to White Balsamic Vinegar, you can use rice wine vinegar or apple cider vinegar.

POTATO RADICCHIO SALAD WITH WALNUT/KALAMATA OLIVE PESTO

INGREDIENTS

- 1¼ cup walnuts, separated
- 2 pounds small red new potatoes or fingerling potatoes
- 2 pounds sweet potatoes
- 1 small head red radicchio, sliced thin into ½ - ¾" slices
- ½ cup olive oil
- 8 ounce jar kalamata olives, drained (reserve liquid)
- ⅓ cup nutritional yeast
- 1 bunch fresh basil
- Sea salt and fresh ground black pepper to taste
- ¼ - ½ teaspoon crushed red pepper flakes (optional, but definitely recommended, if you ask me)

PROCEDURES

Toast walnuts in dry sauté pan over medium-high heat until fragrant. Do not brown. Quickly remove from heat when done and set aside to cool in a bowl.

Cook new or fingerling potatoes in salted water until cooked through but still retain their integrity, slightly toothsome (start checking at 13 minutes). Drain. Do not rinse the potatoes as this will remove some flavor and texture. Remember, however, that they will continue to cook, which is why you want to remove them from the stove when they are still slightly toothsome. Cut potatoes in half or quarters, depending on size. Set aside in large mixing bowl.

Peel sweet potato and cut into small cubes similar in size to the white potatoes. Repeat same process as with new/fingerling potatoes. Add to white potatoes.

Add radicchio and ⅔ cup walnuts to the potatoes, and gently toss to combine.

In blender, add remaining walnuts, Kalamata olives, olive oil, nutritional yeast, basil, salt, black pepper, and red pepper flakes. Process until blended. If pesto is thick, add a scant amount of the Kalamata Olive juice at a time until you reach the desired pesto consistency.

Pour pesto over potatoes, then gently toss to combine.

Refrigerate for 2-3 hours to combine; but can also be served warm immediately or at room temperature.

ROASTED TOMATO & GRILLED CORN CHUTNEY QUINOA SALAD

The salad comes packed with lots of color and is bursting with robust flavors from the smoky nuttiness from the pecans and quinoa, the fragrant punch of fresh herbs, and the sweetness of the tomatoes and corn.

INGREDIENTS

- 2 teaspoons liquid smoke mixed with ¼ cup water
- ⅔ cups pecans, roughly chopped
- 1½ cups tri-color quinoa
- 3 cups unchicken broth
- ⅓ cup plus 1 tablespoon olive oil, separated
- 4 cloves garlic, minced
- ⅛ cup plus 1 tablespoon white balsamic vinegar or cider vinegar, separated
- 2 teaspoons unrefined dark brown sugar
- ½ teaspoon dried oregano
- 2 pints grape tomatoes
- 3 ears fresh corn-on-the-cob[*1]
- 1½ cups microgreens or sprouts
- 1 small red onion, chopped
- 3 tablespoons fresh tarragon, minced
- 2 teaspoons mustard
- Sea salt and freshly ground black pepper to taste

PROCEDURES

"SMOKE" THE PECANS

Toss the pecans in the liquid smoke mixture.

Allow to sit and marinate for at least 1 hour, tossing frequently. You can even do this step the day before and allow the pecans to macerate over night for a deeper smoke flavor

Drain pecans and pat dry.

Toast pecans in dry sauté pan until dry and fragrant. Do not burn. Remove from heat and allow to cool in a bowl.

If using whole pecans, roughly chop but keep them in larger pieces.

COOK QUINOA

Rinse quinoa under cool water in a fine-mesh sieve.

Add quinoa to a large saucepan.

Add the unchicken broth.

Cover and bring to a boil, then reduce to a gentle simmer, cracking the lid slightly ajar.

Cook for 15-20 minutes, or until done. When done, quinoa should have become somewhat translucent and have a tail; and water should be absorbed.

Remove from heat, put into a large mixing bowl, fork to fluff the quinoa, and set aside to cool.

ROAST TOMATOES[2]

Preheat oven to 475°F.

Line a cookie sheet with aluminum foil and place in the oven while the oven preheats.

Whisk together 1 tablespoon olive oil, garlic, 1 tablespoon vinegar, dark brown sugar, and dried oregano.

Put a small prick into each tomato using the point of a small knife.

Toss the tomatoes with the marinade.

Remove preheated cookie sheet from the oven and lightly spritz with olive oil.

Pour the tomatoes, including the marinade, onto the cookie sheet, return to oven, and roast in oven for 15-20 minutes, or until done. Tomatoes should take on a slightly charred tone, and begin to pop.

Remove from oven, place the tomatoes in a bowl, and allow to cool.

GRILL CORN

Preheat cast iron grill pan on stovetop, or preheat outdoor grill.

Remove husks and silk.

Using 1 tablespoon olive oil, brush the ears.

Grill until corn is slightly charred and just cooked, but not soft. You want the corn to retain some crunch.

Allow to cool

Cut corn off cob and add to tomatoes.

FINAL STEPS

To the bowl of tomatoes and corn, add the quinoa, pecans, microgreens or sprouts and red onion.

In a small mixing bowl, whisk together the ⅓ cup olive oil, ⅛ cup balsamic vinegar, tarragon, mustard, salt, and black pepper.

Pour dressing onto quinoa/vegetable/pecan mixture, and gently toss to coat.

Refrigerate for at least 2 hours to allow the flavors to meld and complement each other.

Best served at room temperature.

[1] If fresh ears of corn are not available, you can certainly use frozen corn. Preheat a cast iron skillet or similar, add a scant amount of oil, then the corn. Stir until corn takes on a slight char. Remove the corn from the heat and toss with the tomatoes.

[2] You can roast the tomatoes in the air fryer instead of the oven. While you are prepping the tomatoes, preheat the air fryer at 360°F. Lightly spritz the bowl of the air fryer before dropping the tomatoes into the air fryer. Give the tomatoes a quick stir at 5 minutes and 10 minutes. Tomatoes should be nicely roasted in 12-18 minutes, depending on the size of the air fryer.

SPANISH RICE AND BEAN SALAD

This salad is definitely rice and beans taken to a whole new level. While it's meant to be eaten chilled, I have to admit to, oftentimes, not being able to wait as it is mighty fine served warm or at room temperature.

INGREDIENTS

- 3 cups cooked brown rice
- 1 15-ounce can kidney beans, drained and rinsed
- 1 15-ounce can black beans, drained and rinsed
- 1 10 ounce bag frozen organic corn[*1], defrosted
- 1 cup cilantro[*2], roughly chopped
- 2 jalapenos, seeded and minced
- 1 red bell pepper, seeded and diced
- 1 onion, diced
- ⅓ cup olive oil[*3]
- 3 limes, zest and juice
- 2 teaspoons minced garlic
- 2 teaspoons ground cumin
- Sea salt and fresh ground black pepper to taste

PROCEDURES

In a large mixing bowl, gently toss to combine the brown rice, kidney beans, black beans, corn, cilantro, jalapenos, bell pepper, and onion.

In a small bowl, whisk together the olive oil, lime zest and juice, garlic, cumin, salt, and black pepper.

Pour the dressing over the rice and veggies, and gently toss to combine.

Refrigerate for 2 hours before serving.

*1 If it's fresh corn season, use that instead. It will definitely heighten the dish. Cut the fresh, raw kernels off the cob and use. No need to cook the corn. In fact, I definitely recommend against doing so for this salad if using fresh corn. It's such a short season, so let's enjoy it while we can.

*2 Use the leaves only of the cilantro. However, no need to have those lovely stems go to waste. Put them in a blender with some lemon juice, a clove or two of garlic, and a dash of salt. Whiz it up, and you have yourself some mighty yummy cilantro chutney, which would be lovely served alongside your salad or saved for later use as the basis for a dressing to be tossed with salad greens, or served with tortilla chips and guacamole.

*3 Swap out the olive oil with sesame oil and you will have an entirely different taste sensation.

CHAPTER 6
KEEPING IT UNDER WRAPS

A TRIP AROUND THE WORLD THROUGH THE EYES OF A WRAP

Nothing is more universal throughout the world than stuffing a seasoned mixture into some sort of folded wrap, whether it be street food, a dumpling awaiting adornment of a sauce, or a hand-held roll anxiously awaiting being dunked in a complementary dip. We're talking both sweet and savory here.

DOLMAS (DOLMADES)

quintessential finger food, originated in Armenia but is typically associated with Turkey and Greece. Fragrant brown rice and veggies are stuffed in grape leaves then stewed to absolute perfection.

INGREDIENTS

- Two 16-ounce jar grape leaves, drained, rinsed and stems removed
- ½ cup extra-virgin olive oil, separated[*1]
- 1 very large white onion, diced
- 8 scallions, thinly sliced, both green and white parts
- 1⅓ cups finely-chopped fresh dill
- 1⅓ cups finely-chopped flat-leaf parsley
- ⅔ cup finely chopped fresh mint
- 1¾ cups Arborio rice
- 2 teaspoons Better Than Bouillon No Beef Base[*2]
- 2¾ cups water, separated
- Himalayan sea salt and freshly ground black pepper, to taste
- 2 tablespoons fresh lemon juice
- Fresh lemon wedges for serving
- Plain unsweetened yogurt[*3], for serving (optional)

PROCEDURES

After prepping the grape leaves, set aside on a clean kitchen towel to absorb excess water. Cover with a damp clean towel so they don't dry out.

Set a large skillet over medium heat and add 3 tablespoons oil and onions. Sauté until translucent and soft, approximately 5 minutes, stirring occasionally.

Add the scallions, dill, parsley, and mint and continue cooking for an additional one minute.

Add the rice and bouillon, stirring constantly, for 2 minutes. Add 1¼ cups water and cook, stirring occasionally, for 10 minutes, without lid, until the water is absorbed. Rice will not be completely cooked at this point.

Remove from the heat and season with salt and pepper. Set aside until fully cooled.

Line the bottom of a large heavy-bottomed pot or Dutch oven with 3 layers of grape leaves, which will prevent the dolmades from scorching on the bottom of the pot during the cooking process.

Working one at a time, arrange the remaining leaves, bottom-sides up with the points facing you. Place a heaping tablespoon of filling in the center of each leaf, then fold the left and right sides over the filling. Fold the tip of the leaf over the filling, then roll tightly to make a roughly 2-inch by ½-inch cigar shape. Place the roll, seam side down, in the lined pot. Continue with the remaining leaves and filling, placing them tightly together in the pot and continuing onto a second layer as necessary.

Place the pot on the stove.

Bring the remaining 1½ cups of water to a boil.

Add the boiling water, the lemon juice, and the remaining oil to the pot. Bring to a simmer over medium heat, then lower the heat to medium-low and cover the pan; cook until the rice is tender and the leaves are very tender, about 45 minutes.

Remove the pot from the heat and let cool completely.

Serve the dolmades at room temperature or chilled, drizzled with olive oil. Garnish with lemon wedges for squeezing and Greek yogurt for dipping or topping.

*1 If you prefer no-added oil, you can certainly swap out the oil for water or broth. It will alter the flavor and texture somewhat; however, you will still be pleased with the end result.

*2 This is my go-to product for flavored broths. It is sold in small glass jars as a paste. The paste comes in several vegan flavors, such as no beef, no chicken, mushroom, roasted garlic, and vegetable. They do not, however, produce exclusively vegan pastes, so read the labels carefully to ensure that you don't mistakenly purchase the non-vegan product. If you have another favorite, go ahead and use it.

*3 For a more Grecian yogurt, line a colander with cheesecloth and pour the yogurt in the fabric. Allow the yogurt to drain for at least two-three hours, overnight would be better if possible, in the refrigerator. This will produce a thick yogurt. The longer you allow it to drain, the thicker it will become, from a Greek yogurt texture to a Neufchatel cheese if you allow it to drain overnight.

SHUMAI DUMPLINGS

This Inner Mongolian pocket of yumminess is stuffed with scented mushrooms and soy curls as the meaty base with other vegetables, herbs, and spices joining the party. The more traditional method of cooking is in a steamer and served as a dumpling; but you can take it up a notch by pan frying them afterwards ... you then have a potsticker.

INGREDIENTS

- 1 recipe of Shumai filling (recipe to the right)
- 24-28 square wonton wrappers*1
- 2 tablespoons Vegan egg whisked with ⅓ cup water; or ¼ cup Vegan Egg
- 1 recipe of Dipping Sauce (recipe under filling recipe)

PROCEDURES

Remove wonton wrappers from package and set between a clean, damp kitchen towel so they don't dry out while you are working with them.

Using one wrapper at a time, brush the wrapper with the egg mixture.

With your non-dominant hand, make a circle with your thumb and index finger, then lay the wrapper on top. Gently nudge the wrapper down into the circle to create a well for the filling.

Add 2 teaspoons of the filling into the well, then pat the filling down with the back of a small spoon or your fingers.

Fold the overhanging edges of the wrappers down outwardly, leaving the top of the filling exposed.

Press and pinch the wrapper firmly around the filling so that the egg mixture works as a glue to hold it together.

Pat the top and bottom of the dumpling to make it flat.

Optional: Top the filling with a frozen pea and or small piece of carrot. Repeat this process until you have all the dumplings formed.

TO STEAM THE DUMPLINGS:

Line a bamboo steamer or stainless steel steamer with parchment paper that has holes punched through it to allow the steam through; then lightly spritz the parchment paper with oil so the dumplings will not stick during the steaming process.

Arrange the dumplings in the steamer. You want to arrange them in the steamer with a scant amount of room between them to avoid them sticking together during the steaming process.

Put the steamer basket over simmering water in either a skillet or wok, ensuring that the water does not come close to touching the bottom of the steaming pan. Cover.

Steam the dumplings for 8-10 minutes.

*1 There are several brands currently on the market that are considered vegan. Be sure to read the labels because some are made with eggs.

SHUMAI FILLING
INGREDIENTS

- ¾ cup Butler soy curls, reconstituted and drained
- ¾ cup shiitake mushrooms, fresh or already reconstituted
- 4-inch finger of fresh ginger, peeled and grated
- 2 scallions, finely chopped, using both the green and white parts
- 2 tablespoons tamari
- 2 tablespoons plum vinegar
- 1 tablespoon toasted sesame seed oil
- 1 tablespoon plus one teaspoon cornstarch
- Himalayan sea salt and fresh ground black pepper to taste

PROCEDURES

In a small food processor bowl, pulse together the soy curls and mushrooms until ground but still have some texture, like a ground meat.

In a mixing bowl, combine the soy curls/mushrooms mixture with the ginger, scallions, tamari, vinegar, sesame oil, and cornstarch. Season with salt and pepper and combine well.

DIPPING SAUCE
INGREDIENTS

- 1 tablespoon chile paste or sauce
- 2 tablespoons tamari or Namu Shoyu

PROCEDURE

In a small bowl, whisk ingredients together.

VEGETABLE CANNELLONI

This Jersey Italian girl couldn't include a section on wraps without including a trip to Italy. This Italian classic is made gluten-free by using vegetable sheets in lieu of the lasagna pasta.

INGREDIENTS

- Sheeted vegetables (zucchini, butternut squash, potato, eggplant, etc.)*1
- 1 recipe of Spinach Ricotta (recipe to the right)
- Tomato Gravy*2
- ½ to 1 cup Violife, Follow Your Heat Grated Parmesan, or homemade Parmesan cheese*3, optional

PROCEDURES

Preheat oven to 375°F.

Spread a scant amount of gravy on the bottom of a casserole pan that is large enough to fit your cannelloni in a single layer.

To fill the cannelloni, I find it easiest to load the ricotta into a pastry bag with a large piping tip. Working with one sheet at a time, pipe the ricotta down the middle, then wrap the sheet around the filling. If you don't have a pastry bag and tip, you can use a spoon or spatula to line the sheet with the ricotta.

Place seam side down in the casserole pan.

Continue until all cannelloni rolls are in the pan.

Spread more gravy over the top of the cannelloni.

Sprinkle the grated Parmesan sparingly over the top.

Cover with foil and bake for 20 minutes, then remove the foil and continue to bake until heated through and cannelloni shell is tender but not falling apart, approximately an additional 10-13 minutes.

*1 I have found that sheeting butternut squash seems to work best as it is a structurally stronger veggie than the others; however all work well. You might be able to purchase vegetables already sheeted. I use my sheeting attachment for my stand mixer. You can always go more traditional and use manicotti shells or lasagna sheets. If you use lasagna sheets, parboil the pasta for 3 minutes less than the cooking directions, or until the sheets are just pliable. You don't want to overcook them because they will cook further when you bake the cannelloni.

*2 For your tomato gravy (you may be more acquainted with referring to it as "tomato sauce"), make the gravy in the "Sauces" section or take a short-cut here and use a really well-seasoned store-bought jar of sauce.

*3 In terms of store-bought grated Parmesan cheeses, these two would be the only brands that I purchase. You can make your own version of a homemade grated cheese by pulsing together toasted nuts, nutritional yeast, and sea salt.

SPINACH RICOTTA

INGREDIENTS

- 5 ounces fresh spinach
- 1 tablespoon olive oil
- 1 small-medium onion, chopped fine
- 3 garlic cloves, minced
- ¾ cup firm to extra-firm tofu
- ¾ cup raw cashews, soaked and drained
- ¼ cup lemon juice
- 2 tablespoons nutritional yeast
- 1 tablespoon plus 1 teaspoon white miso paste
- 1 tablespoon cornstarch
- ¼ teaspoon fresh ground nutmeg
- Himalayan sea salt and fresh ground white pepper to taste

PROCEDURES

In a dry sauté pan, sauté the spinach until wilted. Remove from heat, strain by putting inside a clean kitchen towel and wringing it to get all the moisture out. Reserve the liquid and set aside. Chop spinach and set aside in a large mixing bowl.

In a small sauté pan, sauté the onions in the olive oil for 2 minutes over medium heat, then add the garlic. Continue to sauté for another 2-3 minutes, or until the onions are translucent but have not taken on any color and the garlic is fragrant. Remove from heat, and set aside to cool slightly.

Add all the ingredients into a blender, and blend until well combined. If the ricotta is too thick, add 1-2 tablespoons of the spinach liquid or water as needed until you reach the desired consistency. (Note: Since we will be mixing this ricotta with spinach, it is best to keep it on the drier, thicker side.)

Remove ricotta from blender. Cover and refrigerate until ready to use.

POTATO CHEESE PIEROGI

My Russian Godparents would be proud of this recipe. Tender, light dough enrobing cheesy mashed potatoes. My Aunt Dot used to make these by the hundreds for the Annual Russian Picnic. It was the highlight marking the end of the summer. We would always go early so that my parents were sure to be able to purchase several dozen to take home. Aunt Dot would boil the pierogies first, then douse them in lightly-sautéed onions swimming in butter. Our vegan version will never have you looking back, I promise.

INGREDIENTS

- 1 recipe Pierogi dough
- 1 recipe Potato Cheese filling
- Serving Option: onions sautéed in a copious amount of butter

PROCEDURES

Bring a large pot of salted water to boil.

Line a large cookie sheet with parchment paper and very lightly dust with bench flour. Set aside.

Have a small bowl of water by your work station for sealing the pierogies.

Working in batches (keeping the parked dough under a damp towel) and using a pasta machine or rolling pin, roll the dough to 1/16" thickness. If using a rolling pin, scantly dust your work area with bench flour. A refrigerated rolling pin, especially a cast iron enameled one, makes rolling out this dough an absolute breeze.

Using a 3" cookie cutter, cut out dough rounds. Reserve trimmings on the side, keeping them under the damp towel to re-roll.

Lightly dampen the edges of the round.

Dollop a heaping tablespoon of filling into the center of a round.

Fold in half, and seal the edges by crimping. Make sure the edges are sealed well so the filling doesn't ooze out during the cooking process.

Place completed pierogies on the cookie sheet. Cover with clean dusted towel.

Gently lower the pierogies into the boiling water using a slotted spoon. Do not overcrowd, so boil 4-6 at a time.

When they come to the top and float, they are done. It should take approximately 4 minutes. Remove them with the slotted spoon and cover to keep them warm.

At this point, they are ready to serve. See some serving options below.

SERVING OPTIONS:

My Godmother used to sauté onions until translucent in butter to make a sauce. Just before serving, she would place the pierogies in a large bowl, then pour the onion sauce over them and sprinkle some minced parsley.

Pan fry the pierogis in butter or olive oil. Serve with sour cream or yogurt, with chives.

I always make extra because, once you boil the pierogis and allow them to cool, they freeze beautifully for use at a later date. You can defrost them in the refrigerator and then reheat in a skillet or drop in boiling water and remove as soon as they come floating up to the top.

TO MAKE THE DOUGH

INGREDIENTS
- 3 cups flour, preferably all-purpose
- ½ teaspoon Himalyan sea salt
- 4-5 ounces cream cheese, at room temperature (preferably Miyoko's Kitchen or Kite Hill)
- ¼ cup avocado oil
- Water to make soft dough

PROCEDURES

Combine flour and salt in a large mixing bowl.

Using a pastry blender (or my favorite utensil, my own fingers), cut the olive oil and cream cheese into the flour until they are combined. It will make the flour coarse, but there's not enough cream cheese to make pea-sized balls as you would expect when making a pie dough.

Starting with 3 tablespoons water, and adding in additional one tablespoon at a time, work water into the dough until it is soft, smooth, and elastic.

On a floured work surface, knead dough 3 or 4 minutes or until elastic.

Cover dough with plastic wrap and refrigerate for at least 30 minutes.

TO MAKE THE FILLING

INGREDIENTS
- 1½ pounds Yukon gold potatoes, peeled and cut into small chunks
- ¼ cup olive oil
- 1 small onion, finely chopped
- ¼ cup nutritional yeast
- ½ teaspoon fresh-ground white pepper
- ½ teaspoon Himalyan sea salt

PROCEDURES

Place potatoes in pot and cover with water to 1" above the top of the potatoes. Bring to a boil, then reduce to simmer. Cook until potatoes are fork tender, approximately 15-18 minutes. Drain, and return to pot.

Add the remaining ingredients, and mash until well combined.

Set aside to cool.

MAKE IT YOUR OWN

No need to just think "potato and cheese". Sautéed cabbage makes for another classic version. Want a sweet pierogi? Any fruit compote or thick fruit stew, with or without some sweetened nut cheese will leave you wanting more. Think of this recipe as a starting point for your own gustatory creativity.

CHINESE EGG-LESS ROLL

The Air Fryer hits the scene, making this roll a healthy version of the Chinese deep-fried, usually made with eggs, wrap.

INGREDIENTS

- 1 recipe filling (recipe to the right)
- 1 package Egg Roll Wrappers*[1]
- 2 teaspoons corn starch
- ¼ cup water
- 1 recipe Sweet and Sour Dipping Sauce

PROCEDURES

Take the egg roll wrappers out of their package and cover with a damp towel while working with them.

In a small bowl, mix the corn starch and water. Set aside. This will be used to brush the edges to make the 'glue' to hold the rolls together.

One at a time, take a wrapper and place it on your work surface with one corner facing you.

If liquid has settled to the bottom of the bowl of the filling, strain it out before using the filling.

Place approximately three tablespoons of filling into the bottom third (closest to you) of the wrapper.

Brush the corn starch mixture on the top two side edges.

Fold the bottom corner over the filling, and pull back to evenly spread out the filling, then roll firmly to the halfway point.

Fold both the left and right side corners snugly over the roll, then continue rolling until the top corners seal the egg roll.

Place on a parchment lined cookie sheet, seam side down, and cover with a damp towel until ready to cook.

Repeat this process until all egg rolls are prepared.

At this point, you can park your egg rolls by freezing them for future use, or fry them now. If time allows, I find that they fry best if you have the time to park them for 20 minutes in the freezer. This helps to set up the wrappers.

Prep your air fryer:

Make sure your basket is clean. If not, wash with warm soapy water and rinse first.

With your basket in the air fryer, preheat the air fryer to 390°F and set for five minutes.

After three minutes, remove basket from fryer. Using a clean paper towel, quickly wipe or spritz basket with coconut or avocado oil.

Return basket to the air fryer for remaining 2 minutes.

Your air fryer is primed and now your egg rolls will not stick to the basket.

Depending on the size of your basket, plan to air fryer 3-4 egg rolls at a time. You do not want them touching; and you want to allow the air to readily flow around them, thus frying them.

Place 3-4 rolls in the air fryer.

Air fry for 10 minutes, rolling over halfway after the first five minutes.

Remove from the air fryer and serve with Sweet and Sour Dipping Sauce or dipping sauce of your choice.

TO MAKE FILLING

INGREDIENTS

- 1½ cups water mixed with ⅓ cup Vegan Egg; or 1¾ cup Just Egg
- 4 teaspoons avocado oil, separated
- 1 small-medium head cabbage, finely shredded
- 2 large carrots, julienned fine
- 1 cup dried shitake mushrooms, rehydrated and thinly sliced
- 1 cup bean sprouts
- 1 8-ounce can bamboo shoots, shredded
- 3 scallions thinly sliced
- 2 tablespoons Chinese Five Spice (recipe below)
- 1 tablespoon Namu Shoyu
- 1 teaspoon Himalayan sea salt
- 1 teaspoon unrefined cane sugar
- 1 tablespoon corn starch

PROCEDURES

In a skillet, heat 1 teaspoon oil, then pour the egg mixture into skillet. Cook, stirring, until it begins to firm up; then let it cook on one side for 3-4 minutes before flipping and continuing to cook for an additional 3-4 minutes. Remove from pan and allow to cool. Slice into thin strips. Set aside.

Heat the remaining oil in a large wok. Stir in the cabbage and carrots and cook until they begin to wilt, 2-3 minutes.

Add the mushrooms, bean sprouts, bamboo shoots, scallions, Chinese Five Spice, Namu Shoyu, sea salt, cane sugar and corn starch. Continue cooking until all vegetables begin to soften, approximately 6 minutes.

Stir in the sliced Vegan Egg.

Spread mixture onto a large cookie sheet, and allow to cool in the refrigerator for at least one hour before making egg rolls.

*1 There are several brands currently on the market that are considered vegan. Be sure to read the labels because some are made with eggs.

CHINESE FIVE SPICE

INGREDIENTS

- 2 teaspoons ground cinnamon
- 2 teaspoons anise seeds or 2 star anise, ground
- ½ teaspoon fennel seed
- ½ teaspoon freshly ground pepper
- ¼ teaspoon cloves

PROCEDURES

If using whole spices, grind to a powder in a coffee grinder.

If using ground spices, combine all powders together.

Store in glass jar in cool cabinet.

WINTER ROLLS

Raw earthy veggies show up wrapped in brown rice paper in this exquisite, opposite-of-a-summer-roll representation from Thailand. Served with Indian Cilantro Chutney, Parsley Cashew Sauce, or Peanut, it makes for a fabulous appetizer but is hearty enough to serve as main dish.

INGREDIENTS

- ⅓ cup tahini
- 1-2 tablespoons water
- 4 teaspoons Namu Shoyu, separated
- ½ teaspoon sea salt
- ½ pound organic, non-GMO sprouted firm tofu
- ¼ pound black bean thin spaghetti or similar
- 1 large, or 2 small, raw red beets, peeled and shredded
- 2 carrots, raw and shredded
- 1 cup butternut squash, shredded
- Dash of sea salt and garlic powder
- ½ cup scallions, minced
- 12 brown rice paper wraps
- 1 Recipe of Parsley Cashew Dipping Sauce, Peanut Sauce, or Indian Cilantro Chutney

PROCEDURES

In a small food processor or blender, combine the tahini, 2 teaspoons Namu Shoyu, and sea salt with just enough water to make a viscous sauce. Set aside.

Drain the tofu, then dry it in a tofu press or clean dish towel to take out liquid. You want the tofu as dry as possible.

Julienne the tofu, then marinate in the remaining 2 teaspoons Namu Shoyu for 1 hour.

Lay out the tofu in a single layer on a parchment-lined cookie sheet, then bake in a preheated 375°F oven for 15-20 minutes, or until dried and lightly browned. Do not overcook, as they will dry out. You want the tofu to remain moist inside with outer edges that are slightly crisp.

Cook the black bean spaghetti according to package directions, ensuring that the pasta remains slightly al dente. Drain and rinse until cool, then toss with ⅓ of the tahini sauce. Set aside.

Using a julienne vegetable peeler, process the beets and carrots in julienne strips. Set aside.

Using the julienne vegetable peeler, process the butternut squash into julienne strips. Optional, but my preference: in a skillet, lightly sauté the squash until it just begins to slightly wilt. Remove from heat. Sprinkle with a dash of sea salt and garlic powder, then set aside.

Once you have completed all the above mis-en-place, you are ready to assemble your wraps. You will need to work quickly with each rice paper wrap while being careful not to tear it. You want to work on one roll at a time, from start to finish, before moving on to the next roll.

Put warm water in a bowl that is large enough to easily fit one sheet of rice paper flat in the bowl. Have a couple of clean dish towels lined up.

Take one sheet of rice paper, place in the bowl of warm water, and gently move about until it becomes slightly supple.

As soon as it is supple enough to work with, take it out of the water and place on a clean dish towel, lightly drying it off.

Put a thin line of the tahini sauce down the center of the rice paper.

In the lower third of the wrap, place ½ of the following ingredients: black bean spaghetti, tofu, beets, carrots, butternut squash, and scallions. You want to leave a one-inch clean edge while spreading out the ingredients evenly in a row.

Fold up the bottom ⅓ of the roll to seal in the ingredients. You want to make sure that this first roll is taut before continuing on to the next step. You can do this by gently pulling the roll towards you while keeping taught the unrolled portion.

Next, you want to fold in both sides, again ensuring that you are keeping the ingredients taut inside the roll.

Finish rolling the wrap away from you until the rice paper is completely wrapped.

This sometimes takes a little practice, but once you get the hang of it, you will be good to go.

You'll want to serve these immediately or cover them securely so that rice paper does not dry out.

Cut the wrap in half on a cross-angle and place on the serving platter. The cutting on a cross-angle adds to the presentation.

Serve with Parsley Cashew Dipping Sauce, Peanut Sauce, or Indian Cilantro Chutney for dipping.

SERVING OPTION:

Wrap a second rice paper skin around the roll for sturdiness, then place in a pre-heated air fryer at 390°F for 10 minutes for a cooked version with a crispy exterior and warm, textureous interior.

DESSERT BOLLO WITH CRÈME ANGLAISE

This slightly sweet dessert is better known as a Tamalé in Mexico, Humita in Bolivia, and Bollo in Colombia. The unexpected surprise is that rather than a savory stuffing enveloped with masa, our version has a sweet stuffing and slightly sweetened masa before wrapping it in a corn husk. Served in the corn husk slit open with a generous drizzle of vanilla crème angleise, this Bollo will alter how you will forever think of a Tamalé

INGREDIENTS

- 2 cups chopped nuts
- ¼ cup maple syrup or agave
- ⅔ cup avocado oil
- 1 tablespoon cinnamon
- 1 tablespoon crystallized ginger, minced
- ¼ teaspoon nutmeg
- ¼ teaspoon cloves
- ¼ teaspoon allspice
- 1 teaspoons sea salt
- 1 teaspoon baking power
- 2 cups masa, adding a little at a time
- 1½ to 2 cups simple syrup*1, warmed
- 12 corn husks

PROCEDURES

In a mixing bowl, mix the nuts and maple syrup together. Set aside. This will become the filling.

Separate corn husks and put the whole large ones in a large pot. Cover with warm water, and place a dish on top so they stay emerged. Soak for 10-15 minutes, or until they soften. Remove them from the water, dry, and keep stored as you're working with them between damp towels so they don't dry out.

In a large mixing bowl, whisk together the oil, cinnamon, ginger, nutmeg, cloves, allspice, sea salt, and baking powder.

Using a wooden spoon, mix in the masa.

Add the simple syrup, mixing well, adding more, a little at a time, until mixture resembles a soft dough.

Spread a thick layer of the masa on the inside of a softened corn husk. Dollop 3 tablespoons of the nut mixture in the center of the masa.

Fold tamale so that the masa and filling remain in the center by folding in a side at a time until you have a sealed packet.

Layer Bollos in a steam tray, seam side down.

Bring water in steamer to a simmer. Place the steam tray with the Bollos in the steamer.

Cover and steam for 1½ - 2 hours.

Remove from heat.

Serve the tamales, opened, with Crème Angleise.

*1 To make simple syrup, combine equal parts water and sugar. Whisk to combine over low heat until sugar is completely dissolved. Remove from heat and allow to cool. Make extra simple syrup as it is wonderful to sweeten cold drinks, such as iced tea or lemonade.

CRÈME ANGLAISE

INGREDIENTS

- ¼ cup water mixed with 1 tablespoon Vegan Egg; or ¼ cup Just Egg
- ½ cup cane sugar
- 1 teaspoon cornstarch or potato starch
- 1⅔ cup boiling milk (soymilk of full fat coconut milk work best)
- 1 tablespoon vanilla extract or paste

PROCEDURES

In a mixing bowl, begin to beat the egg mixture.

Gradually add the sugar to the egg mixture. Continue beating for another 2 to 3 minutes, until the mixture forms a pale yellow ribbon.

Beat in the starch.

While you continue beating the 'egg mixture', gradually pour in the boiling milk. You definitely do not want to rush this step. If you do, you may end up with lumps that you'll have to strain out later.

Once it is all combined, pour the mixture into a saucepan, and over medium heat, continuously stirring until the mixture begins to coat a spoon. Unlike making pudding, you do not want this to come to a simmer or a boil. You are looking for a viscous sauce that will pour when cooled versus a pudding that will set up.

Remove from the heat, and continue to beat sauce for another minute or two to facilitate cooling the Crème Anglaise without it forming a stiff layer on the top.

If necessary, strain through a fine sieve.

Stir in the vanilla.

Serve warm.

At this point, you can park the sauce, once cooled, in the refrigerator. Line the top of the sauce with a piece of waxed paper. When you are ready to serve, gently warm the sauce on a double boiler until just warmed through. Do not allow it to come to a boil.

SERVING OPTIONS:

Keep it sweet, but change up the filling. Try a spiked fruit compote, such as cherries with kirsch, apricots with Gran Marnier, or apples with rum.

Not feeling like making the Cremé Anglaise? No worries. Serve with a scoop of vanilla ice cream, and possibly even a drizzle of melted chocolate.

Switch it up to a more traditional version by using a savory stuffing, such as a thick Bolognese, molé black beans, or vegetable stew.

CHAPTER 7
THE MAIN EVENT

**COMFORT-INSPIRED ENTREES SURE
TO HEARTEN AND ENLIGHTEN
ONE'S SOUL (AND PALATE)**

These main course offerings will take you out of the humdrum doldrums and will expand your 'go-to' repertoire for nightly meals.

BEEF WELLINGTON WITH MUSHROOM SPINACH STUFFING AND BROWN GRAVY

If you want to impress your guests with a main dish, this is the one for you. Don't be alarmed or intimidated by the list of ingredients. Planning ahead makes this Wellington incredibly easy because you can make it in segments over the course of several days, even parking the stuffing and/or the roast, without the pastry wrap in the freezer for a future event.

ROAST INGREDIENTS

ROAST - DRY
- 2 cups vital wheat gluten
- ¾ cup garbanzo bean flour
- ¾ cup nutritional yeast
- 1 tablespoon onion powder
- 1 tablespoon smoked paprika
- 2 teaspoons kala namak (black salt)

ROAST - WET
- 1½ cups beefless broth
- ½ cup tomato sauce
- ¼ cup namu shoyu
- 2 tablespoons olive oil
- 1 tablespoon tomato paste
- 2 teaspoons liquid smoke

BOILING
- Cheesecloth
- 4 cups broth

EN CROUTE
- 1 tablespoon avocado oil
- 1 package vegan puff pastry

ROAST PROCEDURES

In a large stand mixer with a dough attachment, gently whisk together the Roast dry ingredients.

In a large cup, mix together the Roast wet ingredients.

With the mixer on low speed, gradually pour the wet ingredients into the dry ingredients until a dough forms, then increase speed to high and knead for 5 minutes. If the dough is sticky, add a scant amount of vital wheat gluten and knead more to tighten.

Cover with a damp, warm, clean towel.

Allow the dough to rest for 5-10 minutes.

On a clean surface, roll the dough out into a long rectangle. You may need to sprinkle a scant amount of vital wheat gluten flour or garbanzo bean flour so that the dough will not stick (but only a sprinkle).

Spread out the stuffing on top of the dough, leaving a 2" perimeter all around.

Carefully roll the dough so that you have a long log*1. Seal the seam and sides by folding and crimping together.

Wrap the roast snugly in the cheesecloth, tying closed.

Bring the boiling broth to a rolling boil in a large heavy stockpot that has at least 3"-4" headroom, then carefully place the roast into the pot. Bring it back to a boil, cover, and reduce to simmer. Cook for one hour.

Turn the stove off, and allow seitan to sit in the broth for 15-30 minutes before removing.

Allow the roast to cool on a wire rack for at least 20 minutes before removing the cheesecloth.

Allow the roast to cool completely on wire rack before proceeding further. Note: You can do this step, and park your roast in the refrigerator or freezer for future use.

Preheat oven to 450°F.

If the roast has been in the freezer or refrigerator, allow it to come to room temperature before proceeding.

In a large skillet, heat the avocado oil. Brown the roast on all sides in the skillet, then set aside to cool.

Open the puff pastry, and gently roll over the pastry to remove the folds, being careful to not roll the pastry thinner.

Place the cooled roast in the middle of the pastry. Fold the sides of pastry to enrobe the roast completely, pinching the pastry seam together and folding the sides to seal.

Place the wellington seam side down on a parchment lined cookie sheet.

Slit the top of the pastry to allow the steam to escape.

Bake in oven for 10 minutes, then reduce heat to 425°F and continue baking for an additional 20-25 minutes, or until puff pastry is golden brown.

Remove from oven and allow to rest for 8 minutes before serving/slicing.

Serve with warmed gravy.

*1 A bench scraper can help you lift the dough and keep the log even as you roll it.

STUFFING

INGREDIENTS

- 1 medium onion, chopped finely
- 2 teaspoons olive oil
- 4 garlic cloves, minced
- 1 teaspoon fresh rosemary, minced
- 1 pound baby spinach
- 1 cup dried mushrooms, chopped
- 1 cup nutritional yeast
- 1 teaspoon fresh thyme, minced
- 1 teaspoon fresh oregano, minced
- ½ teaspoon smoked paprika

PROCEDURES

In large sauté pan, sauté the onions in the oil until almost translucent. Add the garlic and continue to sauté until the garlic is fragrant. Do not caramelize.

Add the rosemary, and sauté until fragrant.

Add spinach, and toss until spinach is wilted.

Add the mushrooms and toss until moisture begins to be absorbed. If there isn't enough moisture from the spinach to rehydrate the mushrooms, add a very scant amount of water, just enough to allow the mushrooms to hydrate and become supple.

Add the nutritional yeast.

Add thyme, oregano, and paprika, tossing to combine well.

Remove from heat, and set aside to cool.

GRAVY

INGREDIENTS

- 1 large onion, chopped fine
- 3 tablespoons avocado oil, separated
- ¼ cup white whole wheat pastry flour
- 3 tablespoons dried shitake mushrooms, ground to a powder in a spice grinder.
- 2 cups beefless broth
- Sea salt and fresh ground black pepper to taste

PROCEDURES

In saucepan over low heat, caramelize the onions in 2 teaspoons oil, approximately 20-25 minutes. Be patient and you will be justly rewarded. This is where you will get a large part of your flavor.

Sprinkle in the flour to coat onions.

Add the remaining oil, and stir to combine well and remove any lumps.

Continue cooking until the flour is gently brown but not burned.

Add the mushroom powder, and stir to combine.

Pour the broth into the saucepan, stirring/whisking to combine well.

Continue to cook over medium heat until the gravy thickens and begins to simmer. Continue to simmer for additional 2 minutes.

Pour in gravy boat.

COQUILLES ST. JACQUES À LA PROVENCALE

King oyster mushrooms swap out for scallops, which are simmered in white wine and herbs, then gratinéed with homemade Swiss cheese. Julia (as in Julia Child, my childhood idol) would have served this course with either a chilled rosé or a fine French dry, white wine.

INGREDIENTS

- ⅔ cup minced onions
- 5 tablespoons butter, separated
- 3 tablespoons minced shallots[*1]
- 3 cloves garlic, minced
- 4 large King Oyster Mushroom Stems, cut width-wise into ¾" slices (approx. 24 slices)
- 1 teaspoon Fleur de Sel sea salt
- ½ teaspoon white ground pepper
- 1 cup sifted flour[*2] in a bowl
- 1 tablespoon olive oil
- 1 cup white vermouth[*3] or dry white wine
- 3 tablespoons water
- 2 bay leaves
- ¼ teaspoon dry or ½ teaspoon fresh thyme
- 24 scallop shells (aluminum or ceramic), buttered and set in a single layer on a cookie sheet
- ¼ cup Swiss cheese, grated (recipe to the right)
- 4 tablespoons butter, formed into a log, refrigerated, and cut into 24 rounds

PROCEDURES

Sauté the onions in 2 tablespoons butter until soft and translucent without adding any caramelization. Stir in the shallots and garlic, and sauté for an additional minute, until fragrant. Set aside.

Sprinkle the 'scallops' with the salt and pepper.

Dredge the scallops in the flour, then shake off excess flour.

In a large skillet, sauté the scallops in the remaining 3 tablespoons butter and the oil for 2 minutes to brown them lightly. Turn, repeat on other side. To ensure that you are able to brown the scallops rather than steam them, do not crowd the pan. Work in batches to accomplish this task.

When all the scallops are browned, add the vermouth, water, bay leaves, and thyme to the skillet along with the scallops. If needed, add an additional tablespoon of water.

Add the onion mixture.

Cover the skillet and simmer for 5 minutes.

Uncover the skillet. If there is a lot of liquid, boil down rapidly until sauce is lightly thickened. Remove bay leaves. Adjust seasoning (salt and pepper).

Place one scallop in each scallop shell, and add some sauce over each scallop.

Top each scallop with 1 teaspoon of Swiss cheese, and then top each with one butter round.

At this stage, you can park the scallops in the refrigerator until you are ready to broil them.

Heat the scallops in a preheated 450°F oven for 3-4 minutes, until they are heated through, the butter has melted, and the cheese begins to brown.

OPTIONAL, BUT RECOMMENDED

After removing them from the oven, use a kitchen Crème Brulee Kitchen Torch to lightly brown the cheese.

Serve immediately.

[*1] If you don't have fresh shallots, freeze-dried shallots work incredibly well.

[*2] If you are gluten-intolerant, a gluten-free flour will work just as well as wheat flour.

[*3] Not all Vermouth is vegan. The brand that was easiest to source and is vegan is Tribuno Dry Vermouth.

SWISS CHEESE

INGREDIENTS

- ½ cup raw Brazil nuts, soaked for at least 4 hours, then drained and rinsed
- 1½ cups water
- ¼ cup nutritional yeast
- 3 tablespoons fresh-squeezed lemon juice
- 2 tablespoons tahini
- 1 tablespoons onion powder
- 1 teaspoon dry mustard
- 1 teaspoon garlic powder
- ¾ teaspoon sea salt
- ¼ teaspoons ground coriander
- 1½ tablespoons agar agar powder

PROCEDURES

In a blender, process the nuts, ½ cup water, nutritional yeast, lemon juice, tahini, onion powder, mustard, garlic powder, salt, and coriander until homogeneous and smooth. Park in the blender.

In a saucepan, whisk the agar agar powder in the remaining 1 cup water. Let it bloom for five minutes, then bring to a boil over medium high heat. Lower to a simmer, whisking often (almost continuously), for five to eight minutes. You will notice a change in the consistency of the mixture.

Quickly transfer the agar mixture into the blender with the remaining ingredients and process until smooth and homogeneous.

Pour into a container, and allow the cheese to set in the refrigerator, uncovered, for two to four hours. Using a spring-form pan for this step really helps.

Remove the cheese and wrap in waxed paper. Store in a sealed container in the refrigerator. While this cheese will last in the refrigerator for 1 to 2 weeks and will continue to age, I would make ahead and allow it to age in the refrigerator for at least two to three days before using.

MOLÉ BLACK BEAN STEW WITH MANGO STICKY RICE

A generous scoop of Mango Sticky Rice with a liberal ladle of the Molé Black Bean Stew is sheer perfection as a hearty dinner but even better for serving a crowd—such as a Super Bowl Party. Complimentary side offerings could be the Tomato Mango Lime Salsa and Cashew Crema.

MOLÉ BLACK BEAN STEW

INGREDIENTS

- 5 cups dried black beans, soaked overnight with a small piece of kombu*1
- 2 mulato chilies rehydrated in 1 cup hot water (or any other dried chili of your liking)
- 2 pasilla chilies rehydrated in 1 cup hot water (or any other dried chili of your liking)
- 1-2 tablespoons avocado oil
- 1 large onion, chopped
- 8-10 garlic cloves, minced
- 1 12-ounce bottle of chocolate or coffee infused stout or ale
- 2½ cups strong Coffee*2
- 12 cups flavorful broth, chickenless or beefless preferred
- 1 tablespoon dried epazote*3, crushed
- 1 tablespoon annatto paste
- 1 jalapeno, minced
- ½ cup Mexican Chocolate*4
- Additional broth or water, if needed
- 1 recipe Mango Sticky Rice (follows below)
- 1 recipe Cashew Crema
- 1 recipe Tomato Mango Lime Salsa

PROCEDURES

Soak black beans at least 8-12 hours in water with kombu. When you are ready to begin cooking, drain and set the beans aside, tossing the kombu and soaking water.

Soak Mulato and pasilla chilies in the hot water for 15 minutes, then puree and set pureed mixture aside.

In large heavy-bottomed stock pot, sauté the onions in oil on medium/low heat, until they are slightly caramelized, approximately 15 minutes.

Add the garlic, and continue sautéing until fragrant.

Add the stout/ale, coffee, broth, epazote, annatto paste, and jalapeno.

Bring to a boil, then reduce to a simmer. Stir at least once every 15 minutes.

Cook for 3-4 hours, or until the black beans are soft and the stew is thick.

Stir in the Mexican chocolate so that it melts completely and is thoroughly combined.

Optional: Garnish with a healthy dose of chopped scallions and/or cilantro.

NOTE

Once the liquid becomes viscous from the starch in the beans, you may want to lower the heat slightly, but keep it simmering; and stir more often, to prevent sticking on the bottom of the pan. If you need more liquid, add a scant amount of additional broth or water to keep the bottom of the pot from scorching.

*1 Kombu is magic when used in the soaking as well as the cooking water for dried beans. It helps to remove the "musicality" that is often associated with eating beans.

*2 You can also use a grain beverage, such as Coffig - use the equivalent of 4 tea bags in hot water, allow to steep at least 1 hour before using.

*3 Epazote is a rather pungent herb that is used in Mexican cuisine. Honestly, it smells rather akin to old, dirty gasoline, at least that's what it makes me think of. However, when used during cooking beans, it's positively supernatural. You can purchase it dried in most stores where they sell dried Mexican herbs. I actually have some growing in my garden, but beware. It is a rather invasive perennial that will take over, similar to mint. So I have mine growing in its own pot. If you are using fresh epazote, you'll want to use 1.5 times the amount.

*4 Mexican chocolate is typically lightly sweetened and has cinnamon in it. If you don't have Mexican Chocolate, you can use ¼ cup dark chocolate chips, and then add ¼ teaspoon cinnamon.

MANGO STICKY RICE

INGREDIENTS

- 2½ cups organic brown jasmine rice
- 4 cups 100% Mango Juice
- 1 13.5-ounce can coconut cream
- 1 13.5-ounce can coconut milk of your choice
- 2 cups water
- Fruit from 2 mangoes plus ¼ cup water, pureed

PROCEDURES

Put all the ingredients (excluding the pureed mango/water mixture) into a large, heavy-bottomed stock pot.

Bring to a boil, then reduce to a gentle simmer.

At the beginning, you'll want to stir about every ten to fifteen minutes.

Once the mixture begins to become viscous, reduce the heat to barely simmering and stir every five to ten minutes. You want to make sure that it doesn't stick to the bottom and burn.

It will take approximately 1 hour 20-25 minutes from start to finish.

When it's done and creamy, stir in the mango puree mixture.

Best served warm or at room temperature.

Optional: If serving as a side in a serving dish, sprinkle with cinnamon for an added punch of flavor.

CAJUN-INSPIRED MEATLOAF

This isn't my mother's meatloaf that was smothered with ketchup on top. Oh no! (Sorry, Mom) This is a marvel that was inspired by one of my favorite dishes from a New Jersey restaurant that has long since closed. Packed with lots of veggies and other whole plant foods, you'll want to add this dish to your go-to repertoire. And while you're at it, you'll probably want to double the recipe so you can freeze a loaf or two for future meals.

INGREDIENTS

- 6½ to 8 cups beefless broth, separated
- ⅔ cup lentils, dried
- 1 cup brown rice, uncooked
- 4 tablespoons avocado oil, separated
- 2 cups diced onions, separated
- 1 cup diced red pepper
- 1 cup chopped celery
- 2-3 jalapenos, finely chopped
- 2 cups textured vegetable protein, dried (or butler's soy curls, minced fine)
- 1 cup pecans, chopped finely but leaving texture
- ½ cup sesame seeds
- 1 teaspoon fresh ground black pepper
- 1½ cup barbeque sauce (recipe follows)
- ½ cup VeganEgg powder or ½ cup Flaxseeds, ground to a powder
- 8 ounces tomato juice
- ¼ cup Namu shoyu
- 1 cup shredded cheddar cheese

PROCEDURES

Preheat oven to 300°F.

In a pot, bring three cups of broth to a boil. Add the lentils, cover, reduce to a simmer, and cook until lentils are tender, about 30 minutes. If broth remains, drain. Lentils should still be slightly chewy. Set aside.

In another pot, sauté the rice in 1 tablespoon oil on low heat until the rice takes on a golden color. Stir often. This is an important step for the flavor, so don't rush it.

Add 1½ cups broth to the rice. Bring to a boil, cover, and reduce to a simmer. Simmer for 30-35 minutes. Rice should still be somewhat al dente. If there is still broth remaining, uncover, and reduce, stirring so that the rice does not burn. You don't need to reduce all the broth. Set aside.

In large sauté pan, sauté one-half the onions on medium-low heat in the remaining oil until caramelized, approximately 25 minutes. Again, do not rush this step as you want to bring out the flavor of the caramelization process in the onions without burning them.

Add the rest of the onions, red pepper, celery, and jalapenos. Cook until tender, approximately five minutes.

In large mixing bowl, add the lentils, rice, cooked vegetables, textured vegetable protein, pecans, sesame seeds, black pepper. Toss to combine. Set aside.

In a blender, mix the barbeque sauce, VeganEgg powder or ground flax seeds, 2 cups broth, tomato juice, and Namu Shoyu together.

Pour the liquid mixture into the lentil/rice/TVP mixture, and stir to combine.

Knead and then allow the mixture to stand for five minutes to help TVP to reconstitute. If the mixture still feels crunchy, add additional broth, a scant amount at a time, until the TVP is no longer crunchy but the mixture is not soggy wet.

Place in a baking dish that is lightly spritzed with oil. Cover with foil and bake for one hour, or until center is cooked.

Remove foil and top with your favorite vegan shredded cheddar cheese. Broil or brulee until cheese is melted.

Serve with Spicy Chili Sauce (recipe follows) on the side.

BARBECUE SAUCE

INGREDIENTS

- 1 cup tomato sauce
- ½ cup tomato paste
- ¼ cup light brown sugar
- ¼ cup cider vinegar
- ½ teaspoon liquid smoke

PROCEDURES

In a sauce-pot, whisk all ingredients together, then bring to a simmer over medium heat. Reduce heat to a gentle simmer, and cook for 10 minutes.

SPICY CHILI SAUCE

INGREDIENTS

- 1 medium onion, chopped
- 2 tablespoons oil
- 1 bell pepper, chopped
- 1 jalapeno pepper, minced
- 1 stalk celery, chopped
- 1 large can crushed fire-roasted tomatoes
- 1 teaspoon coriander, ground
- 1 teaspoon cumin, ground
- Sea salt and fresh-ground black pepper to taste

PROCEDURES

Sauté onion in the oil until soft and translucent.

Add peppers and celery, and sauté until vegetables are tender, approximately 4 minutes.

Add the tomatoes and spices, and cook for additional ten minutes.

Season with sea salt and freshly-ground black pepper.

TOURLOU – GREEK RATATOUILLE

A variety of vegetables that frequently show up in Greek cuisine are braised to create a hearty entrée that is both colorful and piquant.

INGREDIENTS

- 2 cups shelled and cooked fava beans*1
- ¼ cup olive oil
- 2 medium onions, thinly sliced
- 1 medium-sized fennel bulb, chopped (retain and set fronds aside)
- 2 large red potatoes, cut into ½-inch slices
- 6 multi-colored carrots, sliced into bite-size pieces
- 2 small eggplants, peeled and sliced into bite-size pieces
- ⅓ cup thinly sliced scallions
- 2 teaspoons fennel seeds, freshly ground
- 1 cup Pinot Grigio or Sauvignon Blanc wine
- 1¾ cups unchicken broth
- 2 cups frozen baby artichokes, thawed and cut in half
- ½ preserved lemon, rinsed and cut into strips
- 2 tablespoons capers (if in liquid, drain; if in salt, reduce salt to ½ teaspoon)
- 1 teaspoon sea salt
- 1 teaspoon fresh ground black pepper
- 6 tablespoons fresh lemon juice, separated
- 2 teaspoons cornstarch
- 1 cup of mixed fresh herbs (fresh oregano, mint, dill, and/or basil)

PROCEDURES

In a large sauté pan or wok, heat olive oil, then add the onions. Cook 5-6 minutes, or until translucent, not browned, stirring frequently.

Stir in chopped fennel and potatoes. Cook for another 5-6 minutes, stirring frequently.

Add the carrots, eggplants, scallions, and fennel seeds. Stir to combine. Cook for another 5-6 minutes, stirring frequently.

Add the wine and cook 1-2 minutes to begin reducing the wine.

Add the broth, artichokes, preserved lemon, capers, salt, and pepper. Bring to a boil, then reduce to a gentle simmer, cover, and continue cooking for an additional 10 minutes, or until the vegetables are tender but retain their shapes.

Whisk together 3 tablespoons lemon juice with the cornstarch in a small bowl, stirring until smooth. Add the slurry to pan; increase heat back to high, and cook for 2-3 minutes, or until sauce thickens.

Stir in remaining 3 tablespoons lemon juice and the fava beans. Cook for another 1-2 minutes, to heat fava beans through.

Pour Tourlou into a large serving bowl or platter, then garnish with the chopped fennel fronds and herb mixture. Serve immediately.

*1 If you are using dried fava beans that still have their skins intact, soak them for 24 hours, then cook in boiling water for 2 minutes. Drain and immediately plunge in an ice water bath. Drain well. Dry/rub them between a clean terry cloth towel to remove the skins. Remove membranes. (If you are using dry fava beans that already had their skins removed, you will omit the steps of rubbing them in between the dry towel and removing the membrane.) Place fava beans in a large pot and fill with cold water. Bring to a boil, then reduce heat to a gentle simmer and cook until favas are tender, approximately 1½ -2 hours. Set aside.

CHESAPEAKE BAY CRABBY CAKES

Hearts of palm create the perfect riff on this Maryland classic. Serve with Horseradish Sauce.

INGREDIENTS

- 2 tablespoons Vegan Egg
- 3 tablespoons water
- ⅓ cup mayonnaise
- 1½ tablespoons Old Bay Seasoning
- 1 tablespoon Dijon mustard
- ½ teaspoon Sriracha sauce
- 14 ounces hearts of palm, drained and roughly chopped
- 1 cup crushed saltines or soda crackers*1
- 1 recipe Horseradish Sauce

PROCEDURES

In a small bowl, whisk together the Vegan Egg and Water. Set aside for several minutes to thicken.

In a large mixing bowl, whisk together the egg mixture, mayonnaise, Old Bay seasoning, mustard, and Sriracha sauce.

Gently fold in the hearts of palm and crackers. Let stand for several minutes to hydrate.*2

Using a regular-size ice cream scoop, shape into patties, placing them on a parchment-lined cookie sheet. Once they are all formed, park in refrigerator for a least one hour before cooking.*3

Using either the "Cooking in Oil" or the "Air-Frying Method", fry the Crabby Cakes.

To serve, place a crabby cake on top of a piece of endive or loose-leaf lettuce, or baby romaine, and top with a dollop of the horseradish sauce.

COOKING IN OIL

Using a large skillet, cover bottom of skillet with oil.

Once hot, carefully place 3-4 crabby cakes in the oil, and fry on one side for about 3-4 minutes, until golden, before turning.

Flip, and repeat on second side.

Remove from oil and place on paper towel.

AIR-FRYING METHOD

With frying basket or grill pan in place, preheat air fryer for 3 minutes at 390°F.

Quickly spritz basket/grill pan and top of crabby cakes.

Place 3-4 crabby cakes top-side down into air fryer, then give a quick oil spritz to the cakes.

Fry for 8-12 minutes, halfway through spritzing again, then flipping, then spritz the top.

*1 If using salted crackers, check for seasoning. If using unsalted crackers, add salt to taste.

*2 You don't want to break up the texture when you are folding in the hearts of palm and crackers. Fold just until everything is combined. Allowing the mixture to stand will bring it all together.

*3 It's at this point where you can freeze these crabby cakes. Simply place the cookie sheet in the freezer until the cakes are frozen solid. Remove them from the parchment paper and wrap tightly in a sealed container to store in the freezer. When you are ready to cook them, no need to defrost.

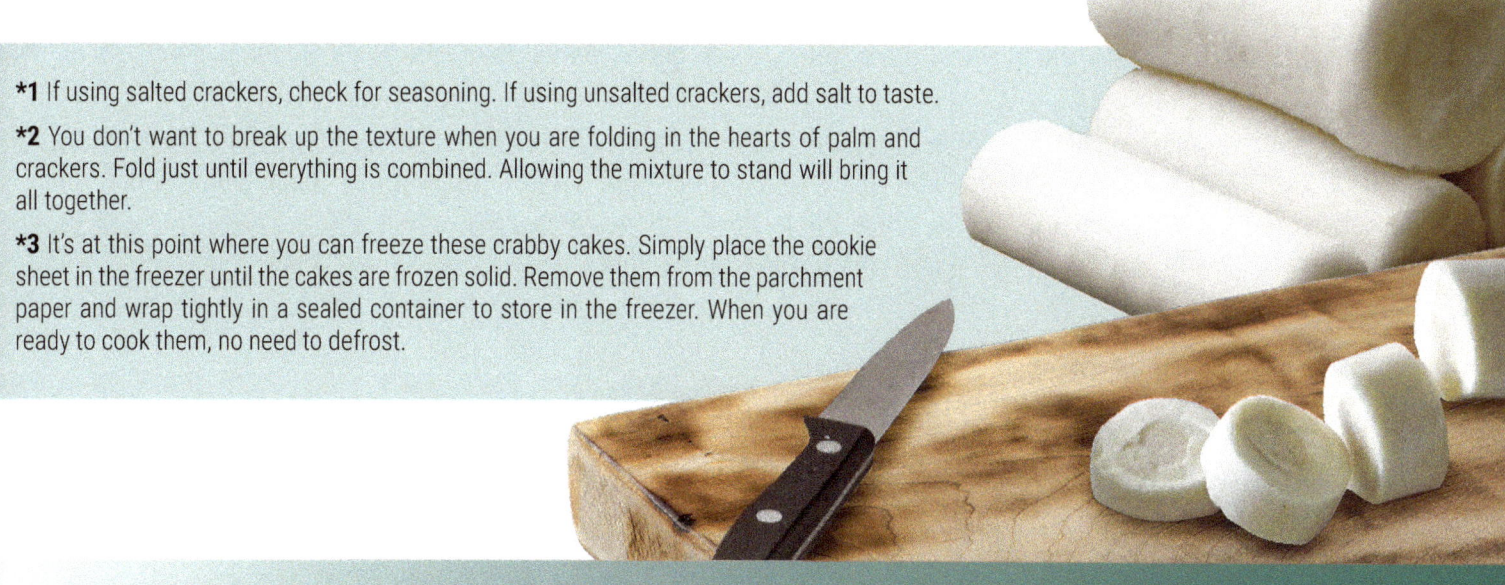

EGGPLANT AND RICE PARMIGIANA

I've not only veganified my family's Italian classic that frequently showed up on the dinner table growing up, I've also lightened it up by eliminating the frying, lessening the amount of cheese (not to mention removing the dairy), and by adding two unexpected, yet complimentary ingredients that will surprise and delight you. This casserole is enough to feed a crowd; but I love making it for an evening meal as the leftovers freeze extraordinarily well. It's always a treat pulling one out of the freezer, reheating it, and serving with a lovely salad. The ideal meal for a busy day.

INGREDIENTS

- 2 cups any combination of raw cashews/almonds/pignolis and water to cover
- 3 tablespoons apple cider vinegar, separated
- ¾ cup nutritional yeast
- 3 tablespoons VeganEgg powder
- 3 tablespoons sea salt, separated
- 3 garlic cloves
- 2 teaspoons onion powder
- 2¾ cups beefless or chickenless broth
- 2 cups Arborio rice
- 2 bay leaves
- 3-4 Italian eggplants[*1]
- 7 cups tomato gravy
- ½ cup loosely-packed, coarsely chopped basil
- 2 cups mozzarella
- 1½ cups shredded Parmesan cheese

PROCEDURES

At least 4 hours before, place the nuts and 2 tablespoons vinegar in a large bowl, then cover with water. After their soaking time, drain and rinse the nuts. Put the nuts, the remaining vinegar, nutritional yeast, VeganEgg, 2 teaspoons sea salt, garlic cloves, and onion powder in a blender. Process, adding water as necessary, until you reach the consistency of thick ricotta. Set aside.

In a medium saucepan, bring the broth to a boil. Add the rice and bay leaves, cover, and reduce to a simmer. Cook until the broth is absorbed, approximately 10-12 minutes. The rice will still be al dente.

Remove the bay leaves, and spread the rice out into a thin layer on a cookie sheet to cool. Set aside.

Peel the eggplants[*2], then slice into ¼-inch thick slices. Sprinkle the remaining salt onto each slice of eggplant, then set them in a colander, with a weight on top of them, to drain for at least ½ hour to 1 hour. Rinse the eggplant to remove the excess salt, and pat dry using a clean dish towel.

Stir the basil into the tomato gravy. Set aside.

In a large mixing bowl, gently mix together the ricotta and rice. Set aside.

In a bowl, toss together the mozzarella and Parmesan cheese. Set Aside.

Preheat oven to 375°F.

Begin assembling the casserole in a 10"x14" casserole dish. Start with a thin coating of gravy to line the bottom of the pan. Line a single layer of eggplant, followed by gravy, then the rice/ricotta mixture, and a scant amount of sprinkled mozzarella/Parmesan, then gravy. Repeat until all ingredients are assembled. End with sprinkling of mozzarella/Parmesan.

Cover with foil and bake for 25 minutes, then remove foil and baked until golden on top and bubbling.

[*1] Use eggplants that are not so bulbous as they tend to have more seeds.

[*2] I always, without exception, peel my eggplants. The skin is tough and never yields courteously to a fork; so in my opinion, it ruins an otherwise stellar meal. The peel does, however, go well in your compost.

BUTTERNUT SQUASH COCONUT CURRY STEW WITH TEMPEH

A hearty main dish with Thai overtones. Perfect for a cool night's dinner paired with cardamom-scented basmati rice.

INGREDIENTS

- 2½ cups unchicken broth, separated
- 1 8-ounce package tempeh
- 2 teaspoons potato starch
- 2 teaspoons plus spritz of olive oil, separated
- 2 teaspoons sesame seeds, ground
- 1 teaspoon cumin
- 2 teaspoons coriander
- 2 teaspoons curry powder
- 5 cloves garlic, finely chopped
- 1 inch finger of ginger, grated or micro-planed
- 2 teaspoons fresh lemongrass, minced very fine
- 2 teaspoons Thai red chili paste
- 2 tablespoons tomato paste
- 1 teaspoon sesame oil
- 1 15-ounce can coconut milk
- ¼ cup Namu Soyu
- 1 small butternut squash, cut into bite-size cubes
- 1 medium-large sweet potato or yam, cut into bite-size cubes
- 3 carrots, cut into bite-size rounds
- 1 medium red bell pepper, sliced
- 1 large onion, thick-sliced
- 10 Brussels sprouts, cut in half
- 1 15-ounce can garbanzo beans, drained[*2]
- 1 bunch cilantro, chopped and separated

PROCEDURES

PREPARE THE TEMPEH[*1]

Place 1 cup unchicken broth in InstantPot and set to 'Sauté' with lid off. This will dramatically reduce time it take to bring to pressure.

While heating the broth, cut tempeh into bite-size pieces, then add to the InstantPot.

Turn off InstantPot and place the lid on the pot.

Set to 'sealing' or 'pressure', and set the time to zero minutes. The InstantPot will come to pressure and beep when done. Do a 'quick release', and open when able to do so.

Drain tempeh and pat dry.

Coat tempeh with potato starch until it is all absorbed.

Give a quick spritz of oil to the tempeh.

Air fry the tempeh at 360°F for 10-12 minutes, or until golden brown on the outside.

Remove, cut into bite size pieces, and set aside.

PREPARE THE BROTH

In a small bowl, make a thick slurry (using water), with the sesame seeds, cumin, coriander, and curry powder. Set aside.

In a Dutch oven or heavy-bottomed soup pot, sauté the garlic in 2 teaspoons olive oil for 1 minute, then add the ginger, sautéing for another minute.

Add the spice slurry, lemongrass, and chili paste. Sauté for another minute, until fragrant.

Add the tomato paste, and stir to combine. Sauté for another minute to remove the rawness of the tomato paste.

Add the remaining 1½ cups unchicken broth, sesame oil, coconut milk, and Namu Shoyu. Stir until blended, then bring to a gentle rolling boil.

COMPLETING THE STEW

Add the butternut squash, sweet potato, carrots, bell pepper, and onions.

Bring back to a gentle boil, cover, and reduce to simmer.

Cook until veggies are toothsome (al dente), approximately 20-28 minutes, depending on how large you cut the squash and potatoes.

Add the Brussels Sprouts and tempeh, and cook for additional five minutes.

Add the garbanzo beans.

Stir in the cilantro just before serving, leaving some for garnish.

Place a scoop of basmati rice into a bowl.

Ladle the stew around the rice.

[*1] I have found that tempeh resists accepting a marinade throughout it. But when you treat it in this fashion, you will be delighted and amazed how well the marinade has seeped through and permeates the tempeh.

[*2] Save that garbanzo bean liquid, aka Aquafaba for another use, such as baking the Italian Pignoli Cookies or the Mini Roasted Red Pepper Quiche.

ETHIOPIAN-SPICED ROASTED ROOT VEGETABLE TART

A mélange of Ethiopian-perfumed roasted root vegetables baked in a rustic, free-form tart crust.

FILLING

INGREDIENTS

- 1 tablespoon olive oil, separated
- 1½ cups butternut squash, diced into small cubes*1
- ¾ cup carrot, diced into small cubes*1
- ¾ cup leeks, chopped*1
- ¾ cup red bell pepper, chopped*1
- ¾ cup cauliflower, chopped*1
- 1 tablespoon berbere*2
- 1½ teaspoons sea salt
- 1 teaspoon ground cumin
- 1 teaspoon ground coriander
- ½ teaspoon ground allspice
- ½ teaspoon paprika
- ¼ teaspoon black pepper, ground

PROCEDURE: PREPARE THE FILLING

Preheat oven to 375°F with a 9"x12" baking dish in the oven.

In a large bowl, combine 2 teaspoons olive oil with all the other filling ingredients.

Remove the baking dish from the oven. Working quickly, lightly coat the bottom of the dish with the remaining oil, and evenly spread the vegetables in the dish.

Cover with foil, return the pan to the oven, and roast the vegetables until they are fork-tender, about 35-40 minutes.

Remove the pan from the oven, place the vegetables in a bowl, and allow them to cool. If there is any residual oil in the oven pan, do not carry that over into the bowl.

CRUST

INGREDIENTS

- 1½ cup white whole wheat pastry flour plus additional bench flour, refrigerated
- ¾ butter, cold and cut into cubes
- 6 ounces cream cheese, cold
- ¾ teaspoon sea salt

PROCEDURE: PREPARE THE CRUST

While preparing the crust, preheat the oven to 400°F.

In a food processor (helpful if bowl and blade have been refrigerated for at least one hour), pulse the crust ingredients until they begin to come together in clumps, approximately 15-20 pulses.

Dust a cool work surface with a scant amount of bench flour, then dump the dough onto the work surface. Knead gently until the dough comes together. Do not over-knead.

Using a large sheet of parchment paper, roll the dough into approximately a 16-inch circle about ⅛" thick. Remember, this is a rustic tart, so perfection is not necessary.

Transfer the dough, keeping it on the parchment paper, onto a large metal pizza pan.

ASSEMBLAGE

INGREDIENTS
- ½ cup herbed cheese spread, separated
- 1 tablespoon nutritional yeast
- 3 tablespoons Vegan Egg, separated
- ¼ cup water (may need a slight bit more)

PROCEDURE: ASSEMBLAGE

Roll out the dough in a round that is approximately 1/4" thick.

Spread one-half of the herbed cheese spread onto the crust, leaving a 1½-inch border.

In a small bowl, mix the nutritional yeast, 2 tablespoons Vegan Egg, and water together. If mixture is too thick, add a scant amount of water.

Toss yeast/egg mixture into the vegetables.

Spoon the vegetable mixture onto the crust, again leaving the 1½-inch border.

Dot the vegetable mixture with the remaining herbed cheese spread.

Fold up the border of the crust, creating pleats, over the edge of the vegetables.

Mix the remaining 1 tablespoon Vegan Egg with 2 tablespoons water. You may need a slight amount more water as you are creating an eggless wash.

Brush the crust with the egg wash.

PROCEDURE: BAKING

Bake until the crust is golden brown, approximately 35-45 minutes.

Allow to cool and set for at least ten minutes before serving.

Cut into wedges.

Optional: Serve with a dollop of sour cream or plain unsweetened yogurt.

*1 *You want the vegetables to all be as symmetrical as possible.

*2 Berbere is an Ethiopian spice blend that typically contains chili peppers, coriander, garlic, fenugreek, ginger, basil, as well other spices, which are less familiar, such as, korarima (aka Ethiopian cardamom), rue, ajwain, nigella, and radhuni.

SMOKY KALE AND POTATO CASSEROLE

This was my favorite dish that my Dutch Grandma Voorhis used to make. Of course, back then, she made it with bacon, lots of butter, and even more cream. My vegan version brings Ahimsa to the plate without sacrificing any flavor. Double the recipe, and make a huge casserole. Air fried leftovers in the form of tater tots or patties the next day are something to look forward to, I promise.

INGREDIENTS

- 1 pound kale, stripped of the stems
- 1½ teaspoons liquid smoke, separated
- 3-4 pounds yellow potatoes, peeled and cubed
- 1 small onion
- 1 8-ounce tub of cream cheese
- 1 cup milk, preferably soy or almond, unsweetened and unflavored
- 1 cup shredded Parmesan Cheese
- 1 cup mozzarella cheese
- Sea salt and fresh-ground black pepper to taste

PROCEDURES

Preheat oven to 375°F.

In a large stock pot, steam the kale with water and 1 teaspoon liquid smoke until kale is tender. Drain kale and squeeze in a clean dish cloth to release the liquid*1. Coarsely chop the kale and set aside.

Place the potatoes in a stock pot and cover with water. Carefully poke a copious amount of slits in the onion, then add to the pot. Cover and bring to a boil over medium-high heat, then remove lid, and reduce to simmer. Cook until the potatoes are fork tender, approximately 20 minutes. Remove from heat, remove and discard onion, drain potatoes. Return them to the pot.

Add the cream cheese and milk. Mash potatoes, but leave some texture. If needed, add some additional milk; however, remember that the kale will exude some additional moisture.

Stir in the remaining smoke, kale, Parmesan and mozzarella cheeses.

Season to taste with salt and pepper.

Using a scant amount of olive oil, sparingly coat a casserole dish.

Spread kale and potato mixture into the casserole pan, spreading evenly.*2

OPTIONAL: dot with butter.

Bake in the oven until warmed throughout and top has begun to slightly brown, approximately 25-30 minutes.

*1 Reserve the kale pot liquor as an addition to future stocks.

*2 At this point, you can park the casserole in the refrigerator until you are ready to bake. It also freezes well at this point

BEATIFIC BEET BURGERS

I have a fun story about the why and how I created this recipe. Back some time ago, I began a long-distance relationship with a man who was an omnivore. It was going to be the first time that he visited me, so of course, I wanted to impress him with my culinary prowess. I asked him what his favorite foods were; and his response was, "I can tell you what I don't like. I HATE beets!" So, me being me, I knew immediately what that meant to me. Translated, I had to come up with a recipe that included beets that I would serve him for the first meal upon his arrival. After much pondering, I figured that beets would impart sort of beef-like color to a plant-based burger. So, off I went, testing and tasting, until I landed with this recipe. I served these burgers on my English Muffins with lettuce, tomatoes, onion slices, and homemade ketchup. After he finished devouring every morsel while exclaiming his delight, I informed him that he could no longer say that he didn't like beets. While the relationship didn't last, at least this recipe was/is a keeper.

INGREDIENTS

- ⅓ cup raw cashews
- 3 large red beets, peeled and chopped in 1" diced cubes
- 2 tablespoons plus 1 teaspoon avocado oil
- 2 cups water, separated divided into 1½ cups
- ½ cup green lentils
- ½ cup bulgur wheat*1
- ½ cup onions, minced
- 1 cup mushrooms, minced
- 2 teaspoons fresh thyme, or 1 teaspoon dried
- 1 teaspoon fresh rosemary, minced, or ½ teaspoon dried
- 1 teaspoon salt
- ¼ teaspoon pepper
- 1 tablespoon olive oil for frying burgers

PROCEDURES

Prepare the cashews by presoaking them in water for at least two to four hours. Drain and set aside.

Preheat oven to 400°F with a cookie sheet in the oven*2

In a bowl, toss the beets in 2 teaspoons oil.

When the oven and cookie sheet are preheated, carefully remove the hot cookie sheet out of the oven, and spread the beets evenly in a single layer on the baking sheet. Roast for 20 minutes or until tender. Remove the beets from the oven and set aside to cool.

While the beets are roasting, combine the lentils with 1½ cups water in a small pot on the stove. Bring to a boil, then reduce heat, and simmer for 30 minutes, or until the lentils are tender.

Also on the stove in a small pot, bring the remaining ½ cup water to a boil. Add the bulgur wheat, turn off the heat, and cover for 10 minutes. The bulgur wheat should absorb all of the liquid and be tender when done.

Heat the remaining two teaspoons olive oil in a large skillet over medium high heat. Add the onions, mushrooms, thyme, and rosemary and cook for about 6 minutes. Both onions and mushrooms should be softened.

Now that you have all of your ingredients prepped and ready, you can start forming your burgers.

Place the cashews in either a food processor or Vita-Mix, and process until they become partially blended. Add the beets, bulgur wheat, onion/mushroom mixture, salt, and pepper. Process until combined. Add the lentils and continue processing until everything has combined but still on the chunky side.

Divide the mixture into six burger patties. While not necessary, at this point and if time allows, I prefer to park the burgers in the refrigerator for at least 2-4 hours to firm up (I actually find that freezing them first is oftentimes even better to get a nice sear on the outside so the burger stays intact with each bite). Both methods will help them hold together and sear on the outside.

Heat the remaining one tablespoon of oil over medium-high heat, then carefully cook on each side for about 5 minutes, until golden and crispy.*3

*1 You can substitute millet and/or quinoa.

*2 Preheating the cookie sheet in the oven stops the beets from sticking to the pan during roasting. If you would like to eliminate the oil, swap out the oil for water or broth; and have the sheet of parchment paper at the ready when you remove the hot pan from the oven. Quickly line the cookie sheet with the paper, then spread the beets in a single layer and follow the remaining procedures.

*3 You can also use the air fryer to fry these burgers by preheating the fryer at 360°F for two minutes before placing the burgers into the fryer in a single layer, ensuring that there is ample room between each burger to allow the air to flow freely around each patty. Spritzing the burgers slightly with a scant amount of oil before frying them will aid in their searing. You can also bake them in the oven at 400°F for 12-18 minutes, depending on if they are fresh or frozen.

SOURDOUGH PASTA

One of my new skills that I am still working on is creating a viable sourdough starter. There are a plethora of recipes online to choose from, but I opted to use the recipe from the website, theperfectloaf.com, for the first 7 days. I used the starter and pulled off some amazing homemade pasta! You can use whatever die suits your fancy. So far, I've made both rigatonis and bucatini, which is a long strand of pasta with a hole running down in the inside center.

The results nearly blew me away … Absolute scrumptiousness! Whether cooked fresh or dried, the pasta retains its shape and is able to be cooked perfectly al dente (slightly toothsome). It can hold its own whether it's adorned with a heartier Tomato Gravy (aka Sauce) or Bolognese, or complimenting a light sauce of lightly sautéed vegetables in a flavorful broth.

Here's what I came up with. The amount of flour you'll use may vary each time you make pasta because everyone's sourdough hydration level differs as well as the dryness of the actual flour and the humidity in your home. If you follow these procedures, you will be assured of a wonderful and tasty pasta each and every time.

INGREDIENTS

- 1 cup water
- 3 tablespoons flax seeds, freshly ground
- 1 cup sourdough starter
- 4½ to 6 cups white whole wheat pastry flour, separated
- 2 teaspoons salt, optional

PROCEDURES

In a mixer with a dough hook, mix the water and flax seeds to combine. Allow this mixture to set for ten minutes.

Add the sourdough starter, 4 cups flour, and the salt.

Starting on low speed, combine the ingredients until they begin to form a ball. Increase the speed to medium, and knead for 3-4 minutes. The dough will be soft and light.

Remove the dough and place it into a large bowl. Lightly place a piece of plastic wrap on top of the dough. This will help the dough to not form a skin and will also allow the dough to rise. Cover with a towel and park on your counter at room temperature overnight or for at least 8 hours.

At this point, your dough will have fermented and risen slightly. Depending on the hydration level of your sourdough starter, you will need to add anywhere between ½ cup to 1½ cups additional flour. Start by sprinkling ¼ - ½ flour on a clean, cool, smooth surface. Turn the dough onto the flour and knead the flour into the dough. Continue adding more flour ¼ cup at a time until you have a stiff, yet still quite pliable, dough that will easily go through the pasta machine but will not be sticky. Remember, you can always add flour, but you can't take any away. So better to err on the side of less flour, if you are not sure, at this point.

Cover the dough with the plastic wrap and allow it to rest for at least 15 minutes. This will provide the dough with the opportunity to hydrate the newly-added flour.

Set up your pasta extruder with the die that you would like to use.

Test the dough by running a small amount through the extruder to see if it flows through easily and without sticking to itself once you cut the dough. If it is still too sticky, add a small amount of flour to the dough, and allow it to rest again before extruding the pasta.[*1]

Depending on the hydration level of your starter and the amount of flour you added, I typically get approximately two pounds of pasta from this recipe.

If you are making a strand pasta — i.e., spaghetti, bucatini, or linguine, using a drying rack makes this task extremely quick and easy.

If you are making a formed pasta — i.e. ziti, penne, or rigatoni, you'll want to have some cookie sheets[*2] lined with parchment paper and a slight sprinkling of corn meal at the ready. As you extrude the pasta, line it in a single layer on the sheets.

It usually takes around 15 minutes to make all the pasta.

To cook fresh pasta, bring a copious amount of salted water*3 to a boil and cook the pasta for approximately 5-6 minutes for al dente, or to your liking.

To cook dry pasta,*4 bring a copious amount of salted water to a boil and cook the pasta for approximately 8 minutes for al dente, or to your liking.

Strain the pasta into la scolapasta (prounounce school-a-bast), a colander. Never, please don't ever, rinse your pasta after it cooks. In doing so, you'll remove all the lovely starch that surrounds your pasta, thus losing texture and definitely flavor.

To dress your pasta in the Italian tradition, return it back to its cooking vessel, add some of the sauce you will be using, and heat through. You can also put the pasta directly into your serving bowl and top with the sauce.

*1 If you prefer to go "old-school" and not use a pasta machine extruder, you can hand roll the dough to make pasta sheets for lasagna or ravioli as well as strands, for example, spaghetti, linguine, fettuccine, or pappardelle. Taking a golf ball to baseball-sized ball of dough, roll it out so that it is paper-thin. If you are going to make ravioli, roll the dough out to fit your ravioli press or to be able to fold the dough over in half over your filling, then pressing in between each ravioli to seal them before you cut them into their shapes. You have two options for cutting your pasta strands. You can use a sharp knife or a dough cutter. There are a plethora of dough cutters that have between one and five rollers. You can adjust the rollers to the desired width of the pasta you'd like to create. Run the cutter through your dough. Gently toss the pasta with a scant amount of corn meal so that they won't stick together. Another way to cut your pasta strands is once you have the dough rolled out to the desired thickness, gently roll the dough into a log lengthwise. Using a sharp knife, cut the dough into the desired strand widths. Separate the strands and toss with a scant amount of corn meal. Park your pasta either on your drying rack or cookie sheets lined with parchment paper and lightly dusted with cornmeal.

*2 In honor of my Great-Grandma Felicetta, whenever she made pasta, she dried it the old-fashioned way. She would place a clean sheet on the bed and would then sprinkle it with corn meal. When she was ready to cook the pasta, she would gather together what she needed, and allow the rest to continue drying.

*3 Chefs will tell you that the water should taste like the sea—that's when you know that you have enough salt in the water. But, in today's world of minding our sodium intake, you be your own judge. No judgment here.

*4 If you are going to dry some or all of your pasta, you want to make sure that you have it in a single row to dry. It will take at least several hours to completely dry. It is important to ensure that, before you store it in a tightly-sealed container, it is completely dry, lest it will mold. I leave mine out on the counter overnight, covering it with cheesecloth so that the air can circulate to facilitate the drying process.

RIGATONI

BUCATINI

CHAPTER 8
YEAST DOUGHS

SWEET & SAVORY - WORKING WITH YEAST DOUGHS MADE EASY

Once you get the hang of these basic yeast dough recipes, you will delight in changing them up from sweet to savory and visa versa just by changing a couple of the ingredients.

ENGLISH MUFFINS

These are the real deal, chock full of those infamous nooks and crannies. I have successfully made these English Muffins using a gluten-free flour mix as a direct swap out for the white whole wheat flour with stellar results.

INGREDIENTS

- 3½ cups white whole wheat flour*1
- 2½ teaspoons instant yeast
- ½ teaspoon baking powder
- ½ teaspoon sea salt
- 1¼ cups milk
- 1¼ cups lukewarm filtered water
- 2 tablespoons butter, melted
- 1 tablespoon agave, maple syrup, or brown rice syrup

PROCEDURES

Whisk to combine the flour, yeast, baking powder, and sea salt. Set aside.

In a large mixing bowl, whisk together the milk, water, butter, and agave.

Dump the dry ingredients into the wet ingredients.

Using either a mixer with a dough hook (or use the hand mixer but put only one of the two beaters into the mixer, unless your hand mixer has two dough hooks), mix wet and dry ingredients together at high speed until a soft dough forms. It will take about 2 minutes.

Cover the bowl and put in a warm place until it doubles in size and appears bubbly. This step should take about 1 hour.

Preheat a cast iron skillet or griddle on medium heat for 5 minutes.

Spritz the grill pan lightly with avocado oil.

Spritz each ring and place in the grill pan.

Scoop about ⅓ cup of the batter and pour into each ring. Do not overfill, as the dough will rise significantly during cooking.

Cover the pan, and cook for about 4-5 minutes. You will start to see the sides comes away from the rings and begin to dry/lightly brown. Air bubbles will rise to the top and pop, similar to cooking pancakes.

Carefully remove the rings. You may need to run a knife around the edges. You can easily remove the rings by using a set of tongs.

Flip the muffins, cover, and cook for another 4-5 minutes.

Set on wire cooling racks for 5-10 minutes before serving.

NOTES

For best results, use a cast iron griddle or skillet with a lid and four 3-inch round cookie or biscuit cutters without handles. To scoop out the dough, I use a standard-size ice cream scoop that I've lightly spritzed with oil so that the dough will easily slide out of the scoop. You should get a dozen, or a baker's dozen, of English Muffins from this recipe, depending on the rise you attain with the dough.

Do not cut the muffins with a knife. Use a fork and go around the side of the muffin, piercing it all around. Then split the muffin in half using your fingers. This will retain the integrity of those wonderful "nooks and crannies" that the nationally-recognized variety is so well-known for.

*1 If you are making these gluten-free, add 1½ teaspoons Xanthan gum to the flour. This will aid in the elasticity that you lose because of the lack of gluten.

COOKING THE ENGLISH MUFFINS

CHERRY ORANGE PECAN COUNTRY LOAF

This round and crusty loaf is dense and studded with cherries and pecans with a notable fragrant backdrop of orange. While it is a delight as your morning toast with butter, done the Italian way of then dipping it into your coffee. It becomes even more glorious, thinly-sliced, as the bread component to your fruit and cheese platter.

INGREDIENTS

- 1 Recipe of Poolish, prepared one day prior (recipe below)
- 3¾ cups white whole wheat flour
- ½ cup sugar
- 1½ teaspoons salt
- 2½ teaspoons instant yeast*1
- ⅔ cup fresh squeezed orange juice*2
- ¼ cup agave
- 3 tablespoons avocado oil
- 3 tablespoons orange zest*2
- Bench flour
- 1 cup pecans, toasted and chopped
- 1 cup dried cherries
- Bottle spritzer filled with water

POOLISH

INGREDIENTS

- 1 cup white whole wheat pastry flour
- ⅔ cup water @ 70°F
- Pinch of active dry yeast

PROCEDURES

Combine all ingredients in a clean bowl, and mix by hand with a spoon until mixture is smooth. It will be loose and wet. Cover the poolish.

Allow the poolish to ferment overnight at room temperature.

PROCEDURES

In a bowl, whisk together the flour, sugar, salt, and yeast. Set aside.

In another bowl, whisk together the orange juice, agave, oil, and orange zest. Set aside.

Pour the poolish into a large stand mixer with a dough hook, then add the dry ingredients, and top with the wet ingredients.

Mix on low speed until the ingredients begin to combine, then increase the speed to medium until the dough forms into a ball.

Allow the dough to knead in the mixer for two minutes, then turn the dough onto a clean, smooth surface. If the dough feels wet and sticky, sprinkle a scant amount of bench flour, and knead it into the dough. If the dough feels too dry, sprinkle a scant amount of water on the surface and knead it into the dough. You want the dough to be smooth.

Cover the dough with a clean towel and allow it to rest until it is not quite doubled, which should take between 1-2 hours.

Gently deflate the dough, then knead in the cherries and pecans.

Form the dough into a ball, then either place in a floured bread proofing basket or on a parchment-lined baking sheet. Cover loosely with plastic wrap or a warm, damp, clean towel.

Allow the dough to rise again until not quite doubled, about 2 hours.

Begin preheating the oven at 365°F 1½ hours into the second dough rise. Place an oven-proof bowl with 1" of water at the bottom of the oven.

If you used the proofing basket, place a parchment-lined baking sheet over the top, then carefully invert so that the dough is on the baking sheet.

Lightly spritz the dough with water, then place in the oven.

Bake the bread for 45-55 minutes. At 20 minutes into the baking time, tent it with foil.

The bread is done when the internal temperature reaches between 200°F and 210°F.

Remove from the oven, and slide the bread onto a wire cooling rack.

Allow the bread to cool for 25-30 minutes before slicing.

*1 It is important that you use instant yeast for this recipe because you will be mixing the yeast directly into the dry ingredients rather than proofing it in water first.

*2 The average from one medium orange is approximately ¼ cup of juice and 2-3 tablespoons of zest. Before I juice any citrus fruit, I always zest the fruit first. You will need approximately three medium oranges to attain ⅔ cup of juice, with possibly some juice left over; and you will have more zest than what you need for this recipe. You can freeze the extra zest in an ice cube tray with any remaining orange juice. Once frozen, pop them out of the tray and store in a sealed container. You can use them in the future by either defrosting the cube first; or, if you are adding them to a sauce or stew, add the frozen cube directly into the pot while cooking. It will take about five minutes to fully melt and incorporate.

REAL-DEAL LIGHT AND AIRY DOUGHNUTS

When I am craving a doughnut, I am not talking about baked donuts that are more like cake but rather the light, airy, fluffy, almost melt-in-your-mouth doughnut (notice the difference in the spelling) that, yes, is fried in oil. Now, I'm not suggesting that you make these a part of your regular, every-day meal planning. But, when my sweet tooth harkens "doughnuts", it is definitely the yeast doughnuts that wins out every time, without exception. The basic dough can be used to make the standard ring doughnut with the hole in the center, a round filled doughnut, and even a braided twist.

INGREDIENTS

- 6 tablespoons water, between 90°F and 105°F
- 1½ teaspoons active dry yeast
- ½ cup soy or coconut milk
- 2 tablespoons soy or coconut milk yogurt, unflavored and unsweetened
- ¼ cup JUST Egg
- ¼ cup butter, melted and slightly cooled
- 3⅔ cups all-purpose or bread flour, separated
- ¼ cup unrefined cane sugar
- 1 teaspoon salt
- Bench flour
- Avocado oil for frying[*1]
- Coatings and/or fillings for the doughnuts

PROCEDURES

Cut a bunch of 4" squares out of parchment paper or waxed paper. Set aside.

Arrange your oven racks so that there is at least 4" between the two racks. This will be important as you will be using your oven, turned off, as your "proofing box" for the second rise.

In a small bowl, whisk the yeast in the water. Allow it to bloom until the mixture becomes bubbly on top.

In a large bowl, combine the milk, yogurt, egg substitute, and butter, whisking to combine well.

Combine the 3¼ cups flour, sugar, and salt in the bowl of a stand mixer with a dough hook.

Add the yeast water and wet ingredients to the bowl.

Turn the mixer on low speed to combine the ingredients. If the dough appears too wet, add the remaining flour. Once the dough begins to form, you can either continue to knead the bread in the mixer for five minutes, or you can do it the old-fashioned way of kneading it by hand on a clean smooth surface for 10 minutes.

Cover the dough with a clean towel, and allow the dough to rise, doubling in size. This should take approximately one hour.

Place a tray with boiling water at the bottom of your oven. Do not turn the oven on. If you turn the oven light on, it will do double duty to help keep the temperature conducive to proofing dough but will also enable you to see inside the oven as they are rising to determine if they are ready to fry.

Your oven is now set up as a proofing box for the second rise.

Divide the dough in half, keeping one half covered while you work with the other half.

Lightly flour a smooth work surface[*2] and gently knead the half that you are going to work with first.

Using a rolling pin[*3], roll out the dough to approximately ½" thick.

Using a 3" cookie cutter, cut doughnut rounds. If you are making filled doughnuts, move onto the next step. If you are making doughnut rings, use a second, smaller cutter that's approximately 1" diameter to cut the center hole.

As you cut the doughnuts, place each one on one of those 4" squares, then place the doughnuts in a single layer on a

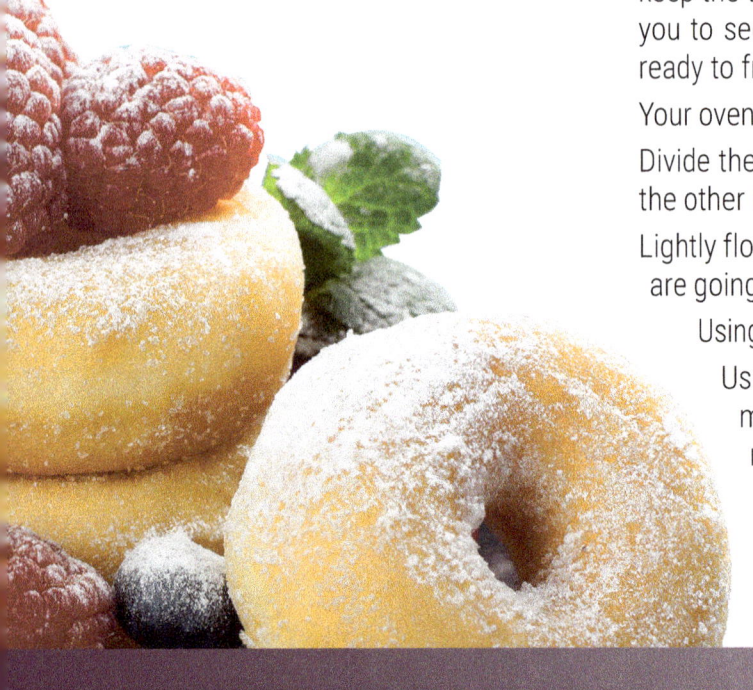

PROCEDURES CONT.

cookie sheet. When you have one tray full, place it in the oven. Repeat this process until you have all the doughnuts cut.

Place the doughnut holes on a separate sheet. If you have any remaining dough, you can cut additional doughnut holes, or lightly and quickly hand-roll the dough to make additional doughnuts for filled doughnuts. That being said, however, you do not want to overwork the dough as the more you work it, the tougher your doughnuts will become.

Allow the doughnuts to rise in the oven until doubled in size, which should take no longer than 45 minutes to an hour.

In a large, heavy stock pot with at least 5"-high sides, bring 2" of oil to 350°F.*4

To fry the doughnuts, turn it onto a spider,*5 removing the paper.

Gently lower the doughnut into the oil, and remove the spider.

Do not crowd the donuts as it will lower the temperature of the oil, which will then give you greasy doughnuts.

As soon as they begin to turn a golden color, use the spider to flip the doughnuts over.

Remove them from the oil as soon as the underside begins to color, placing them on a wire rack or paper-towel-lined cookie sheet to cool.

Repeat this process until you have all the doughnuts fried.

Now comes the fun part – enrobing, dipping, and/or filling your doughnuts.

SUGGESTIONS

Roll the ring doughnuts in sugar, powdered sugar, or a mix of cinnamon/sugar, a mix of cocoa/sugar

Dip one side of the ring doughnuts in a melted chocolate glaze, vanilla glaze, or peanut butter glaze.

To fill the doughnuts, first make a hole in the center of the doughnut using a skewer or chopstick. Fill a pastry bag with a thick vanilla, chocolate, lemon, or coconut custard; flavorful sweet jam such as raspberry blueberry, cherry, or apricot; slightly warmed, but not hot, Nutella so that it will easily flow through the pastry bag, then fill the doughnuts.

*1 You can also use sunflower or grapeseed oil; but my personal favorite is avocado oil.

*2 My preference is a piece of granite or marble. You can sometimes pick up a scrap piece from a counter-top store rather inexpensively.

*3 My absolute favorite rolling pin is my enameled cast iron rolling pin, which is always staged at the ready, parked in the refrigerator.

*4 If you don't have a thermometer, gently lower a doughnut hole into the oil. It should start to immediately fry. If it doesn't, the oil is not yet hot enough. If it turns golden or brown immediately, the oil is too hot.

*5 A spider is a long utensil, usually having a wooden handle, that has a wire mesh, very-shallow bowl at the bottom. It is used to lower and retrieve fried foods out of hot oil. When you go to take the fried item out of the oil, you can lift it up out of the oil and allow the spider to hover over the pot for a couple of seconds, allowing excess oil to drip back down into the pot before moving the items onto a wire rack or draining towels.

GRANDMA MARY'S BREAD LOAF

One of my fondest memories of being in the kitchen with my Grandma Mary was baking this bread with her. She would use her mustard yellow plastic dish pan to mix the dough and then for the first rise. She would guide my little hands over and through the dough as I learned how to knead. And after a while, the magic would happen. Underneath the clean dish towel, the dough rose to double its size. I knew then that I was hooked. I've tried bread machines and used stand mixers with dough hooks to prepare the dough; but I have to admit that I am an old-school girl when it comes to kneading bread dough. I use the best utensils that the universe gifted me with – my hands. And I am always brought immediately back into my Grandma's kitchen with a broad ear-to-ear smile on my face.

So, on to this recipe. Grandma's original recipe was not vegan, of course, and it also made five loaves. I have since converted it to being vegan as well as scaled it down to being able to make one loaf; so, I'm going to give you the measurements for both.

It's a wonderful loaf of basic bread; but Grandma also used it as her foundation for several other variations, which I'll tell you about below.

INGREDIENTS FOR 5 LOAVES	INGREDIENTS	FOR 1 LOAF
3 packages	active dry yeast	½ packages
2 cups	water	¼ cup
5 pounds	all-purpose or bread flour	3 cups
2 cups	milk	½ cup
2 cups	unrefined cane sugar	2 tablespoons
2 tablespoons	sea salt	1 teaspoon
8 ounces	butter, melted	3 ounces
1¼ cups	JUST Egg	¼ cup
scant amount	bench flour	scant amount
spritz	avocado oil	spritz

PROCEDURES

In a small bowl, whisk the yeast in the water. Allow it to proof until the mixture becomes bubbly on top.

In a large bowl, add the flour, then the yeast, water, milk, sugar, salt, butter, and egg substitute.

Mix with a heavy wooden spoon, or use my personal favorite, your hands, to combine the ingredients.

Turn out onto a clean work surface, and knead until a homogenous, smooth dough forms. If the dough feels wet and sticky, sprinkle a scant amount of bench flour, and knead it into the dough. If the dough feels too dry, sprinkle a scant amount of water on the surface and knead it into the dough. You want the dough to be smooth and somewhat elastic.

Lightly spritz the mixing bowl, return the dough to the bowl, roll the dough to lightly coat with oil. Cover the bowl with a clean towel and allow it to rest until doubled. I like to place the bowl in my oven with the oven turned off and the oven light turned on.

Gently deflate the dough.

If you are creating any of the variations*1, now is the time to gently knead them into the dough.

If making one loaf, form the dough into the shape of a log if using a loaf pan, then place the dough in a lightly greased pan. If making five loaves, separate the dough into five equal pieces, and place in lightly greased pans. Cover with clean towel.

Allow the dough to rise again until doubled, approximately 1-2 hours.

Begin preheating the oven at 350°F ½ hour into the second dough rise. Place an oven-proof bowl with 1" of water at the bottom of the oven.

Bake the bread for 35-40 minutes.

The bread is done when the internal temperature reaches between 190°F and 200°F.

Remove the bread from the oven, and allow to cool for 5-10 minutes, then remove the loaves from the pan.

Allow the bread to cool for 25-30 minutes before slicing.

*1 VARIATIONS

For a cinnamon raisin bread, add ½-¾ cup raisins per loaf. Gently flatten out the dough, sprinkle cinnamon (and sugar, optional) over the dough, roll the dough into a log, then place in the bread pans.

Add any combination of dried fruits and/or nuts equaling ½-¾ cup per loaf.

To create a Pannetone, add an additional tablespoon or two of sugar when mixing the dough, then add any combination of candied fruits, such as cherries, citron, lemon peel, orange peel, and/or pineapple to the dough after the first rise. When ready to place in the oven, brush the tops with an egg-substitute wash.

If you want to make a free-form braided round, use the equivalent of two loaves of dough, separated into three pieces. Roll each piece equally in 12"-15" lengths. Braid them together, then create a circle. Where the ends would join, braid their ends together and fold under the loaf. Depending on how large you roll the circle, you can make it a wreath with a hole in the center, or wrap the braid in a circular shape starting at the center and loosely continuing to wrap it around, tucking the loose end under the dough. Place it on a parchment-lined baking sheet, and allow it to have its second rise. You will need to increase the baking time by approximately 10-12 minutes. Start checking after 38 minutes of baking for doneness.

If you want a lighter bread, similar to a Challah, swap out some of the milk for an equal amount of JUST Egg. This bread makes an outstanding French toast.

FOCACCIA

This light and airy Italian semi-flat bread is not only fun to make but is also a brilliant, delectable vehicle for soaking up gravies and sauces left behind at the bottom of your bowl.

INGREDIENTS

- 1 Poolish, prepared one day prior (recipe follows below)
- 4½ cups Double Zero[*1] or bread flour
- 1¾ cups water @ 102°F
- 1 tablespoon Sea Salt
- ⅞ teaspoon active dry yeast
- Bench flour
- ¼ cup Olive Oil, approximately
- 1 sprig rosemary, separated

PROCEDURES

Place the poolish, flour, water, sea salt, and yeast into a large stand mixer set up with a dough hook.

Mix on low speed for a total of six minutes. You will need to stop every two minutes or so to scrape down the sides and bottom of the mixing bowl.

After all the ingredients have been incorporated, increase the speed to medium for an additional minute.

Coat a large clean mixing bowl for proofing (I prefer glass or ceramic) with a scant amount of olive oil, and place the dough into it. The temperature of the dough should be between 75°F-78°F. The dough will be quite loose at this point. Put a slightly damp clean cloth over the top.[*2]

Let it rest for 30 minutes, and then give it one stretch-and-fold sequence[*3].

Perform this stretching/folding sequence four times. Each time, you will notice the dough taking on a more stable and stronger dough-like structure as the gluten develops. Finish the sequence with a 30-minute rest period.

Preheat your oven to 450°F.

Preheat a standard-size cookie sheet by generously brushing the bottom and sides with some of the olive oil. You won't use it all.

Place the entire dough on the baking sheet. Add about 1 tablespoon of the remaining olive oil on top of the dough to prevent your fingers from sticking. Here's where you get to "play the piano" … using your fingers, spread them apart and gently compress the dough outward towards the sides and edges of the pan. No worries if it resists at first, it will eventually yield to your friendly persuasion through the next several steps.

Let the dough rest for 10 minutes, then "play the piano" again, creating a dimpling effect on the top of the dough.

For the next 30 minutes, repeat "playing the piano" at the 10-minute, 20-minute, and 30-minute marks, which will gently coax the dough to finally reach the edges and sides without any effort and without draw-back.

After the second piano play, go ahead and add any desired topping, such as the rosemary.[*4]

After the 30-minute mark, allow the dough to rest for 15 minutes.

Bake the focaccia for approximately 30 minutes.[*5]

When done, take out of oven, immediately remove from the pan, and allow the focaccia to cool on a wire rack before slicing.

POOLISH

INGREDIENTS

- 2½ cups Double Zero or bread flour
- 1½ cups water @ 70°F
- Pinch of active dry yeast

PROCEDURES

Combine all ingredients in a clean bowl, and mix by hand with a spoon until mixture is smooth. (Note: The poolish will be very wet and sticky in consistency. Cover it with a plastic lid or plastic wrap so that there is no air between the cover and the poolish. This will eliminate any skin from developing on the top of the poolish. Allow the poolish to ferment for about 16 hours at room temperature (68-70 degrees Fahrenheit)

NOTE

To keep track of the steps, use my Focaccia Timeline Checklist.

FOCACCIA TIMELINE CHECKLIST

Mix poolish	wait 16 hours
Mix dough	rest for ½ hour
Stretch/Fold #1	rest 30 minutes
Stretch/Fold #2	rest 30 minutes
Stretch/Fold #3	rest 30 minutes
Stretch/Fold #4	rest 30 minutes
	preheat over 450° prepare sheet
Piano #1	rest 10 minutes
Piano #2	rest 10 minutes
Piano #3	rest 10 minutes
Piano #4	rest 15 minutes
Bake @ 350 degrees	Bake 30 minutes
Done	

---

*1 While the bread flour will work just fine, my preference is Double Zero flour.

*2 Since I love kitchen appliances and gadgets but prefer them to not be mono-functional, this is when I pull out my Excalibur dehydrator. I remove the trays and park the bowl of dough with the towel inside. I set the temperature to around 80°F. It works superbly to maintain a steady environment that is conducive to allowing the dough to gently rise.

*3 Stretch and Fold Sequence: Sprinkle a clean dough board with a scant amount of bench flour. Place the dough on the board, then stretch the right end of the dough outward, and then fold it one-third back over itself. Repeat for the left side, then the side in front of you, then the side towards the back. Fold the corners under, then turn upside down and move the dough back into your proofing bowl, covering it with the damp cloth.

*4 You can swap out the rosemary for, or in addition to add, sun-dried tomatoes, olives, capers, etc. However, do not add any cheeses at this point.

*5 If you are going to add cheese, do so after 20 minutes of baking has completed.

NEOPOLITAN-STYLE PIZZA DOUGH

This pizza dough is soft and supple. While you can certainly use the dough as soon as it is ready, I find that it ages perfectly in the refrigerator. You will be really excited with this dough if you have the patience to wait the 48 hours, allowing it to ferment a tad. Make a double batch and store the extra dough balls in the freezer for future use.

INGREDIENTS

- 2 cups filtered water at 105°F-100°F[*1]
- 2 tablespoons sugar[*1]
- ½ teaspoon active dry yeast[*1]
- 5½ cups Double-zero "00" flour (farina)
- 2 tablespoons salt
- 1 tablespoon olive oil
- Spritzer filled with olive oil

PROCEDURES

Combine the water, sugar, and yeast in a bowl. Allow the yeast to proof, until the yeast becomes foamy, about 10 minutes. Set aside.

Mix the flour and salt together in the bowl of a large stand mixer with a dough hook.

When the yeast has bloomed, pour the mixture, along with the oil, into the stand mixer bowl.

Turn on the mixer and slowly combine the ingredients until a dough begins to form. Increase the speed to medium low, and knead for 10 minutes, or you can transfer the loosely-combined dough onto a clean work surface, and knead the dough using your hands.

Transfer the dough into a bowl that is lightly spritzed with olive oil, roll the dough so that it is slightly coated with the oil. Cover with plastic wrap.

Allow the dough to rest and rise for 1 hour.

Divide the dough into 4 balls and place in a 9"x13" greased pan, leaving ample room between each ball. Spritz the dough balls lightly with oil, the cover with plastic wrap.[*2]

Refrigerate 48 hours before using.

[*1] If you have a sourdough starter, you can swap out the water, yeast, and sugar for two cups of sourdough discard to make an equally fine and lovely sourdough pizza dough.

[*2] Alternatively, if you are not going to use all the balls in two days, you can place each of the balls into Ziploc bags that are lightly spritzed with oil. Seal the bags and allow them to ferment in the refrigerator for the two days, then place in the freezer. When you are ready to use the dough, defrost the dough still in the bag, and then allow it to come to room temperature, either in the bag with some air let in to allow for the rise or place in a lightly oiled bowl, before using.

USES FOR THIS DOUGH

PIZZA, BUT OF COURSE

Preheat your oven to 475°F with a pizza stone on the middle rack. If you don't have a pizza stone, you can use a large sheet pan. Roll out your dough, then top with tomato sauce, vegetables of your choice, and cheese. Bake in the oven for 10-15 minutes, until the crust is golden and the topping is bubbling. You can also first grill the dough on your barbecue, flip, then top the pizza. Close the grill lid and allow to grill for a couple minutes, just until the toppings are warmed through.

CALZONES

Roll out the dough in a circle. On one half of the dough, dollop some cashew cheese ricotta, mozzarella, chopped broccoli, and a scant amount of tomato sauce. Fold the other side over the filled half, and seal the edges. Pierce the top of the calzone so that the air can escape during baking. Follow the same baking instructions as the pizza; however, add a couple of minutes to allow the inside to warm through.

PIZZA FRITE

This is a treat that my Grandma Mary used to make with the leftover pizza dough. But, I have to admit, that since I typically keep some dough in the freezer, I make these as a treat whenever the mood strikes. Allow the dough to come to room temperature. Preheat 2 inches of avocado oil to 350°F in a heavy stock pot with at least 4" sides. Put 1 cup of unrefined cane sugar into a clean brown paper bag, and set aside. Cut the dough into small balls, then roll each ball into a strip. Either tie each strip into a knot or make a circle out of each piece. Using a spider, carefully lower a couple of pieces into the hot oil. Do not overcrowd as you do not want the oil temperature to drop, which would cause you to have greasy pizza frite. As soon as they begin to turn golden brown, turn them over using the spider. Remove as soon as they become golden on the other side, and place into the paper bag with the sugar. Give the bag a shimmy shake to coat. Repeat until all the pizza frite is fried and in the bag. Enjoy immediately!

STUFFED BREAD

Preheat the oven to 365°F. Sauté spinach or chopped broccoli in a scant amount of oil with garlic. If there is too much liquid, drain some of the liquid from the pan, especially for the spinach. You can also add some seitan pepperoni or similar. Roll out the dough into an oblong log. Spread the vegetables and/or seitan meat on the dough, leaving a ½" border all around. Sprinkle cheese of your choose. Optional is also dolloping a scant amount of tomato sauce or Alfredo sauce. Roll the dough into a log shape, sealing the seam and the side. Transfer to a parchment-lined cookie sheet. Baked in the oven for 28-35 minutes, or until the bread is golden brown. Remove from the oven and allow the bread to cool before slicing. Serve warm or at room temperature.

CALZONE STUFFED WITH KITE HILL RICOTTA AND GARLICKY SPINACH

CHAPTER 9

SPECIALTY CAKES

CAKES SURELY TO IMPRESS BUT WITHOUT THE STRESS.

The recipes in this chapter can be made ahead in steps and parked, so you can be the hostess with the mostest when your company arrives.

LIMONCELLO COCONUT CAKE

TOASTED COCONUT

INGREDIENTS
- 2 cups shredded unsweetened coconut
- ¼ cup reduced limoncello[*1]

PROCEDURE
Combine the coconut and limoncello together. Spread the mixture out on a cookie sheet so that the coconut can stay in contact with the limoncello. Allow it to macerate for at least 1 hour.

To toast the coconut, you can put it into a dry non-stick frying pan with the heat on medium. Move the coconut about so that it doesn't scorch. When the coconut becomes slightly fragrant and begins to darken, remove from heat and put it on a clean cookie sheet or in a bowl to cool. Another option would be to preheat the oven to 325°F and place the cookie sheet in the oven for approximately 5-10 minutes. This method is a bit trickier because you don't have as much control over the outcome. It is literally only seconds between beautifully toasted coconut and burnt coconut that is only good for the trash.

You can do this step up to several days in advance. To store the coconut, put it in an air-tight container and refrigerate. When you are ready to assemble the cake, take it out of the refrigerator and allow it to come to room temperature.

CUSTARD

INGREDIENTS
- 8 ounces coconut milk (from the can because it's thicker than from the carton and will give you a thick and creamy custard)
- ⅓ cup evaporated cane sugar (or slightly more depending on how sweet you like your custard)
- 3 tablespoons reduced limoncello[*1]
- 2 tablespoons cornstarch or arrowroot

PROCEDURE
Mix all ingredients in a saucepan, and whisk to combine.

Cook over medium heat, stirring constantly, until mixture begins to thicken and bubble.

Stir and continue cooking for additional minute.

Remove from heat and transfer to bowl.

Cover with parchment paper or waxed paper and allow to cool to room temperature.

Refrigerate for at least two hours, or until cool and set, before assembling cake.

CAKE LAYERS

INGREDIENTS
- ¾ cup softened butter
- 1½ cups unrefined cane sugar
- 2 cups unbleached flour (you can use a gluten-free mix, such as Bob's or Pamela's, with excellent results)
- 2 teaspoons aluminum-free baking powder
- ½ teaspoon baking soda
- ¼ teaspoon salt
- Zest of one lemon
- 7.5 ounces silken tofu
- 1 tablespoon avocado oil
- ¾ cup coconut milk (from the carton because it's thinner than the canned milk)
- 3 tablespoons reduced limoncello[*1]

PROCEDURE
Pre-heat oven to 350°F.

Grease, flour, and parchment paper line two 9-inch round metal cake pans.

Using a large bowl with a hand mixer or a stand mixer, beat butter and cane sugar until light and fluffy. This should take about 5 minutes. Set aside.

In another bowl, stir together the dry ingredients: flour, baking powder, baking soda, salt, lemon zest. Set aside.

In a smaller bowl, whisk together the wet ingredients until well incorporated : Tofu, avocado oil, coconut milk, limoncello. Set aside.

For the next 5 steps, it is important to fully incorporate the ingredients in between each of the following steps before moving on to the next step.

Dump ⅓ of dry ingredients into butter/sugar mixture.

Add ½ of the wet ingredients.

Add the next ⅓ of dry ingredients.

Add the last ½ of the wet ingredients.

Add the last ⅓ of dry ingredients.

Pour batter equally in half into the two prepared cake pans.

Bake on center oven rack for 25-30 minutes, or until toothpick comes out clean.

Cool cake layers in the pans on wire racks for 5 minutes.

Remove cake layers from pans, remove parchment paper from the bottom, flip cakes right side up, and allow to cool completely on wire racks before assembling cake.

BUTTERCREAM ICING

INGREDIENTS
- ½ pound Earth Balance Coconut Spread
- 2 cups powdered sugar*2
- 1½ cups tapioca starch or rice flour*2
- ¼ cup reduced limoncello*1
- Pinch salt

ASSEMBLING THE CAKE

On cake dish, put a dab of the buttercream in the center. This will stop the cake from sliding on the serving plate.

Put one cake layer on the plate top-side down. If your cake layers rose with a peak in the center, you might want to level this layer using a serrated-edged knife.

To keep the cake platter clean, put pieces of waxed or parchment paper under the sides of the cake layer. These will be removed after you are done frosting the cake.

On the top of the cake layer, create a small ring of buttercream around the edge. This will help to keep your custard inside the cake and not bleed through your icing on the side of the cake.

Fill the center of your buttercream ring with the custard. You might have some custard leftover. This is for the chef's enjoyment and a preview of what is yet to come.

PROCEDURE

Whip Coconut Spread until light and fluffy.

Add remaining ingredients and mix until the frosty is smooth and creamy.

Refrigerate for at least ½ hour, or until somewhat firmer yet still creamy, before assembling cake.

Top the cake with the second layer, placing it right-side up.

Ice the cake, starting with the top, then the sides.

Sprinkle some of the coconut on the top of the cake, then press it into the sides of the cake. Some will fall off and not stick. You can gather that coconut and continue the process until the entire cake is covered with coconut.

To remove the waxed/parchment paper from the plate, first sweep away as much of the coconut that might have fallen. Then, using a clean knife, run the knife around the bottom of the cake to release the paper from the cake, being careful to not pull the icing off the cake. Clean your knife as you go. Then, using the knife in one hand, gently pull out the piece of paper that is underneath the knife. Use the knife to assist, if needed, to keep the plate clean. Repeat until you have all the paper removed.

Refrigerate at least one hour to set the layers.

---

*1 Over low simmering heat, reduce limoncello to half its volume. Since I use the reduced limoncello in all three aspects of this cake and any unused portions store well in a glass jar, I reduce more than I need. You can use the rest to add to you tea, whether it's hot or cold. But, I'm sure you can come with some other mighty good uses for the leftover reduction.

*2 I really dislike cloyingly sweet buttercream icing, which is why I use a mixture of both powdered sugar and tapioca starch or rice flour. If you are of the ilk that you love a sweet icing, then you can either reduce or eliminate the amount of tapioca starch or rice flour for equal parts confectioner's sugar.

TIP:
Whenever I need citrus zest, I roll the fruit first to help soften the pith inside. Then, using a microplane or zest, I zest the entire piece of fruit. Never being one to waste if I can avoid it, I will then juice the fruit and freeze the juice in an ice cube tray for future use. I'll do the same procedure if I need citrus juice, using the juice and freezing the zest.

HOMEMADE LIMONCELLO

If you really want to impress your guests, you can make your own limoncello. It's incredibly easy; but you'll need to plan ahead – like three months ahead. But trust me, it's so worth it. And you can (and probably should) serve a small shot of the limoncello with each slice of cake you serve. You can serve it straight up (as the Italians would do) or with a spritz of seltzer.

PROCEDURE

The only equipment you'll need is a one gallon glass jug with a lid.

To it, you'll add 3 pounds of organic whole lemons that you've washed and dried. You'll definitely want to use organic lemons as you want to avoid the artificial color that is added to non-organic lemons.

Into the jug, pour an entire bottle (75 ml) of Everclear Grain Alcohol or an equal amount of vodka.

Seal the jug, and set it in a cool, dry, space for a least three months. And wait.

At the end of the three months, the alcohol will have turned a lovely shade of yellow, and the lemons will have released all the juice, rendering them rather hard. The lemons have done their duty, so they get discarded after you strain the liquid.

To the alcohol, add an equal part of simple syrup, which is simply equal parts water to sugar. If you use unrefined cane sugar, it will cloud your limoncello and add a slightly, very slightly, molasses flavor to your limoncello. Otherwise, you'll need to find vegan white sugar as regular table sugar is not vegan (it is processed using bone char to make it that pristine white). Make a large batch of simple syrup, and you can use it to sweeten cold drinks, or drizzle it over fresh berries as a topping for a pound cake or ice cream.

And, Viola! You have homemade, authentic Limoncello.

Now, if you want to stray from Italian authenticity, try making it with limes or oranges (I would suggest using the smallest oranges you can find if you are going to go this route) for a uniquely delightful variation.

ITALIAN SAFFRON RICE TORTA

This indulgent cake truly melts in your mouth with deliciousness! It has the luxuriousness of Arborio rice, saffron, Sambuca, and almonds melded together producing a creamy, yet firm, center. To serve, sprinkle a light dusting of confectioner's sugar on each slice and top with a fanned strawberry for added panache.

EQUIPMENT

- 8-inch springform pan
- Parchment paper
- Butter to grease pan

INGREDIENTS

- 5 cups almond milk
- 1 teaspoon sea salt
- ¼ teaspoon coarsely crumbled saffron threads
- 1 cup Arborio rice[*1]
- ¾ cup granulated sugar, separated
- ½ cup confectioner's sugar
- ½ cup blanched skinned almonds, roughly chopped[*2]
- 2 tablespoons butter or avocado oil[*3]
- 1 tablespoon Sambuca or other anise-flavored liqueur
- 1½ teaspoons lightly mortared anise seeds
- Freshly grated zest of 1 lemon (or orange)
- ⅓ cup unsweetened plain almond milk yogurt [*4]
- 2½ tablespoons Egg Replacer
- ¼ teaspoon cream of tartar
- ½ cup almond, rice, or brown rice flour

PROCEDURE

In a medium saucepan, combine milk, salt, and saffron. Bring just to a boil, then stir in rice. Reduce to a gentle simmer and cook, stirring frequently, until milk is fully absorbed and rice is tender and creamy, about 45 minutes.

Transfer the rice mixture to a large bowl. Stir in ½ cup granulated sugar, confectioner's sugar, almonds, butter, Sambuca, anise seeds, and zest. Park and let cool completely (about 30 minutes) before moving on to the next step.

Heat oven to 400°F with rack in middle.

Grease bottom and sides of the springform pan with butter and line both the bottom and sides with parchment paper.

In a bowl, vigorously whisk together the yogurt, remaining ¼ cup granulated sugar, Egg Replacer, and cream of tartar for 2 minutes. Gently fold into rice mixture until just combined. Do not overmix.

Gently fold rice flour into rice mixture.

Pour batter into prepared pan, spreading evenly with a spatula.

Bake approximately 45 minutes, rotating once halfway through, until dark golden and a toothpick comes out clean in the center.

Cool 15 minutes in the pan on wire rack.

Release cake from the pan.

Serve warm or at room temperature.[*5]

[*1] This is an important ingredient and should not be substituted for another variety of rice. You need to use this starchy rice as it is critical to the texture of your cake.

[*2] If you can't find blanched skinned almonds, don't fret. Place raw almonds in saucepan and cover generously with water. Bring to boil, and simmer for one minute. Strain almonds and drop into an ice bath for one minute. Strain and place the amonds in a clean, dry dish towel. Rub almonds in towel to release the skins. Pop almonds out of skins.

[*3] My preference is definitely Miyoko's cultured butter for this recipe.

[*4] You can substitute another type of unsweetened plant-based yogurt; however, my suggestion is to continue carrying through with the almond flavor.

[*5] If you will not be serving this torta immediately, refrigerate until ready to serve. Remove from refrigerator approximately ½-hour before serving.

DIVINELY-DECADENT CHOCOLATE STOUT CAKE

Trust me on this one. I serve this cake to non-vegan guests, much to their delight and amazement. It is truly worth the effort. A show-stopper, both in appearance and flavor. It is rich and decadent, so thin slices are recommended.

INGREDIENTS

- 2 cups Stout[*1] (preferably a Chocolate Stout, but something like Guinness works well also)
- 2 cups butter
- 1½ cups unsweetened raw cacao powder (I never use cocoa powder, which is quite different and not nearly as chocolaty.)
- 4 cups white whole wheat pastry flour
- 4 cups organic cane sugar
- 1 tablespoon baking soda
- 1½ teaspoons sea salt
- 1 ripe avocado, mashed
- 6 ounces organic firm tofu
- Brewed and cooled coffee or strong cacao mate tea to make 2¼ cups with avocado and tofu
- ⅓ cup Follow Your Heart Vegan Egg Powder
- 27 ounces (2 cans) Coconut Milk (important to use coconut milk from the can and not the carton)
- 27 ounces really-good dark chocolate (can use the vegan dark chocolate chips or chocolate bars chopped)
- 3 eight-inch round cake pans
- Butter or baking spray to coat baking pans
- Cacao powder for dusting baking pans
- Parchment paper to line baking pans

CAKE PROCEDURES

Preheat oven to 350°F.

Coat the inside of the baking pans with butter or baking spray, then lightly dust with cacao powder, shaking out the excess cocoa powder. Line the three baking pans with parchment paper rounds on the bottom of the pans.

Bring the Stout and butter to a simmer using a heavy-duty large saucepan over medium heat. Once simmering, remove from the heat and add the cacao powder. Whisk until the mixture is smooth. Allow mixture to cool while preparing the other ingredients.

Whisk the flour, sugar, baking soda, and salt in a large bowl (dry ingredients) or stand mixer with a large bowl. Set aside.

In a large measuring cup, place the avocado and tofu. Pour in the coffee or mate tea to bring the level up to 2¼ cups. Pour this into a blender, adding the Vegan Egg powder. Blend until smooth.

Keeping the avocado mixture in the blender, add stout/butter/cacao mixture into blender, and blend only until combined. Do not over-process.

Pour mixture from blender into the dry ingredients. Using a mixer on slow/low speed, beat only until combined. Use a spatula to finish fully incorporating batter by folding the batter, scraping the bottom and sides to ensure complete incorporation; but do so only until fully combined.

Divide batter into three equal portions into the baking pans. Here's where having a kitchen scale will come in mighty handily to ensure equal batter because equal batter equals equal baking.

Bake until toothpick comes out clean in the center of the pans; but do not over bake. Depending on your oven, baking can take between 35-45 minutes.

Allow cake layers to cool in their pans on cooling racks for 10 minutes. After the 10 minutes, turn the cake layers out onto the cooling racks and out of the pans. Remove the parchment paper and allow cake layers to fully cool before frosting.

Here is where you can "park" your layers". If wrapped individually, they freeze well, allowing you to space out the tasks.

FOR FROSTING

Put the chocolate chips or chopped chocolate in a large bowl.

Bring the coconut milk to a simmer in a heavy-duty saucepan.

Pour the coconut milk over the chocolate, then whisk until the mixture is smooth and glossy, ensuring that all the chocolate is melted and the mixture is combined. Refrigerate for two hours, whisking every 15 minutes. Once the frosting is thick enough to use, you are ready to assemble your cake.

ASSEMBLING THE CAKE

Line the outer rim of the cake serving plate with parchment paper or waxed paper. This will keep the plate clean while frosting the cake.

On the bottom of the cake plate that you will use for serving, put approximately 1 tablespoon of frosting in the center. This will act as the "glue" to hold your cake in place on the serving plate.

Put your first layer on the plate with the flat side (the bottom of the cake that had the parchment paper removed) facing up. If this cake layer baked with a peak in the center of the top, you might want to use a serrated knife to level it somewhat.

Using an offset spatula, spread approximately ⅔ to 1 cup of frosting on the top of the layer. Repeat this process with the remaining two layers. Refrigerate for 15 minutes to allow the frosting to set up slightly so that the layers won't slip when frosting the outside of the cake.

Using approximately 1½ cups of frosting, lightly frost the top and sides of the layered cake. This is your "crumb coat" that will make the outer frosting layer much easier to complete. Refrigerate for 15 minutes.

Using the remaining frosting, dollop it in the center of the top layer. Using your offset spatula, rotate outward the frosting as you spin/turn the cake plate. This will spread the frosting off to the side of your cake. As the frosting moves to the edge and down the side, guide the frosting down to the bottom of the side of the cake. Once the cake is completely covered, go around the side of the cake with the offset spatula to smooth out the cake.

When you are done frosting the cake, refrigerate for ½-hour.

Run a sharp knife in between the cake bottom and parchment paper only enough to aid in removing the paper off the plate.

Garnish with 3 cherries (stems on) on the top in the center of the cake.

*1 My definitive, absolute favorite stout to use, if you can find it, is Founders Canadian Breakfast Stout. Make sure you buy a couple of extra bottles because it is just as delightful to drink. In fact, you might even serve a small glass to your guests when serving this cake along with a shot of espresso.

PIÑA COLADA UPSIDE-DOWN CORNMEAL CAKE[1]

This is not your ordinary pineapple upside-down cake. Think upside-down cake marries the expected pineapple with the unexpected coconut. Made in a 10-inch cast iron skillet for that Southern authenticity, this recipe truly amps up the coconut with a baker's trifecta (three plus one): Coconut milk, sugar, yogurt, and oil. YUM! (If I can humbly say so myself.)

INGREDIENTS[1]

- ¾ cup coconut milk
- 1 cup coarse ground cornmeal
- 6 slices canned pineapple in its juice[2][3]
- ¼ cup of the juice from the canned pineapple
- 2 tablespoons coconut sugar
- 4¾ ounces white whole wheat flour (it also works equally well with Bob's Red Mill Gluten-Free Flour)
- 2 teaspoons baking powder
- ½ teaspoon salt
- 4 ounces coconut oil
- 8 ounces coconut sugar
- 2 tablespoons dried cranberries plumped in water
- 1 cup coarsely-ground unsalted pecans
- ½ cup plain unsweetened coconut yogurt
- 1 tablespoon coconut oil
- 1 tablespoon plus 1 teaspoon Egg Replacer
- 5¾ ounces coconut sugar
- ½ cup coconut oil, melted and cooled

PROCEDURES

Preheat oven to 350°F with one oven rack in the center of the oven and one directly below it. Place a cookie sheet lined with foil on the rack below the center rack. This will catch any caramel that may boil over during the baking process (and trust me on this one, you definitely do not want to have to clean up spilled over caramel out of your oven). Do not put the cast iron pan and cookie sheet on the same rack as it can adversely affect the air flow and thus, the baking of the cake.

Put cornmeal in a small bowl. In a small saucepan, bring the coconut milk to a boil, then pour over cornmeal. Stir, cover, and let stand 30 minutes at room temperature while you prepare the next steps.

Mix the juice from the canned pineapple with the 2 tablespoons coconut sugar. Over medium heat, melt the 2 tablespoons of sugar in the juice, bring to a boil, then lower to a simmer, and reduce for 10 minutes. Set aside to cool.

Sift together the flour, baking powder, and salt into a medium-sized bowl. Set aside.

In the cast iron skillet and over just-under medium heat, melt the 4 ounces coconut oil, then add the 8 ounces coconut sugar. Stir continuously until the sugar melts, being mindful that the sugar does not go up the sides of the skillet. It will not completely blend with the coconut oil, but will be smooth and glossy.

Take skillet off the heat. Be careful with this step. Hot caramel (your melted sugar mixture) will give you one heck of a burn if it gets on your skin. Gently place one slice of pineapple in the center then place the remaining five slices around the center slice. Place 6-7 cranberries in the center of each pineapple slice. Using a spoon, gently press the cranberries down in the caramel.

Evenly sprinkle the chopped pecans over the top of the caramel and fruit.

Sprinkle the reduced pineapple juice / syrup over the top of the pecans.

In large mixing bowl and with an electric mixer (stand mixer and a hand mixer both work well), beat the yogurt and 1 tablespoon coconut oil until well incorporated. Add the Egg Replacer and beat until well incorporated.

Add the 5¾ ounces coconut sugar to the yogurt mixture, and beat at high speed for at least two-three minutes. The goal is for the sugar to incorporate into the yogurt mix, and for the mix to become light and fluffy.

Add the 1/2 cup coconut oil to the yogurt mixture and beat at high speed until well incorporated.

PROCEDURES CONT.

On medium high speed, mix the cornmeal/milk mixture into the yogurt mixture until well dispersed.

Add the flour mix to the yogurt/cornmeal. Beat at medium-high speed to fully incorporate and complete the cake batter.

Gently pour the cake batter over the fruit and nuts in the cast iron skillet and spread evenly.

Bake in oven for 40-45, until a toothpick comes out clean. Be careful when removing cake from oven.

Cool for 30 minutes in the skillet. This is an important step. Attempting to release the cake too early will cause the cake to fall out in pieces. On the other hand, leaving it in too long will cause the caramel to cool at the bottom of the skillet, causing it to stick and not release. Be sure to be ready to invert the cake out of the skillet at the completion of the 30-minute cooling time.

Run a sharp knife around the sides of the cake in the skillet, being careful not to disturb the cake, but to loosen any caramel from the sides. Place a platter on top of the skillet. Using oven mitts because the skillet will still be quite warm, invert the cake onto the platter and remove the cast iron skillet.

Serve warm or at room temperature.

*1 Typically, ingredients in a recipe are written in descending order by quantity. When an ingredient is to be used twice in a recipe, separated, the total quantity would be listed with "separate" after it. Since this recipe has multiple steps with several ingredients that are used in more than one step, I found this recipe much easier to pull together when I listed the ingredients in components in the order that I would be using each component, and then listing the ingredients within each component in the order that I would be using them.

*2 Swap out the pineapple with peach slices, and make a loose peach puree for the pineapple/coconut sugar mixture, and you'll have yourself a Georgia Peach Upside-Down Cornmeal Cake.

*3 You certainly can use a ripe, fresh pineapple. Cut slices evenly approximately 3/8" thick, and core the center. Juice the remaining pineapple to create the juice to make the syrup.

INDIAN PISTACHIO DATE AND CARDAMOM CAKE

This cake is the perfect accompaniment to end a delightful Indian feast with a steaming cup of masala chai. But, heck, who am I kidding? This cake is perfect for dessert any time. It's truly elegantly delectable for any occasion. Wrapped tightly, is also freezes well to be served at a later date. Simply leave it wrapped while thawing in the refrigerator. Remove from the refrigerator at least one-half hour before serving, and Viola! A dessert that will impress even the most discerning palates.

INGREDIENTS

- 1 pound pitted Medjool dates, approximately 29-31 dates
- 1 cup brandy, cognac preferably
- ½ cup whole unsalted pistachios, shelled
- ¼ cup crystalized ginger, chopped fine
- 1¼ cups white whole wheat pastry flour
- 3 teaspoons freshly-ground green cardamom seeds
- 1 teaspoon freshly-ground coriander seeds
- 6 ounces butter
- ¾ cup organic unrefined cane sugar, ground to a fine consistency
- 5 tablespoons vegan egg powder mixed with ⅝ cup water (add a scant amount more if mixture is too paste-like)
- 2 tablespoons plus 1 teaspoon molasses
- 1½ teaspoons vanilla extract
- ¼ teaspoon Himalayan pink salt
- Powdered sugar
- ½ cup minced pistachios, serving option
- Whipped 'cream', serving option

PROCEDURES

3 days prior to baking: coarsely chop the dates (easiest to do this task in a food processor). Put them into a 32-ounce jar that has a lid. Add the cognac, pistachios, and ginger. Seal the jar and shake until well combined. You'll want to store this jar in a cool, dry place that does not get sunlight. Shake daily, once per day, for 3 days before proceeding to the next steps. Trust me on this one, you won't regret waiting the three days.

On the lower rack of your oven, place a cookie sheet, then add boiling water to the pan.

Preheat the oven to 300°F.

Prepare an 8" round spring-form pan by lightly spritzing the bottom and sides with avocado oil or butter. Then line both the bottom and sides with parchment or waxed paper, ensuring that the paper on the sides extends taller than the pan itself. Set aside.

In a small mixing bowl, whisk together the flour, cardamom, and coriander. Set aside.

In a large mixing bowl (for use in a stand mixer, or a regular bowl with a hand mixer), cream the butter and sugar together until light and airy.

Gradually add in the vegan egg mixture in two parts, between in between each to ensure that they are well combined.

Add the molasses, vanilla, salt, and combine well.

Add the brandied fruit and pistachio mixture and using a slower speed, combine well.

Add the flour mixture in several increments, while beating on a slow speed between each addition to ensure it is well combined.

Once all the ingredients are combined, raise the mixer speed to high and beat for ten-fifteen seconds.

Pour the batter into the prepared springform pan. Gently smooth the top.

Open the oven door and add some more boiling water to the cookie sheet, if needed.

Put the cake into the oven.

Bake for 3 to 3¼ hours, turning once halfway through the baking process. Other than this, which requires you to open the oven door, resist opening the door again until you hit the 3-hour mark. The cake is done when you can put a skewer all the way down to the bottom of the cake, and the skewer comes out clean.

When it is done, remove the pan from the oven and allow it to cool completely on a wire rack before removing it from the pan.

Remove the cake from the pan; however, keep it covered with waxed paper or parchment paper until you are ready to serve to keep the cake moist.

When you are ready to serve, remove the paper covering. Place cake on a serving platter.

Lay a paper doily on the top. If you don't have a paper doily, fold a piece of paper over and over in fan-like folds, then cut very small shapes into the edges. Unfold, and you will have a makeshift doily.

Gently sprinkle powdered sugar on the top. Carefully remove the doily so that it leaves a powdered sugar design.

Optional: Serve with a dollop of whipped 'cream' with a light sprinkling of the minced pistachios atop the whipped 'cream'.

CARROT CAKE WITH CREAM CHEESE FROSTING

This recipe does double duty. Use it to make a luscious carrot cake; but you can also use it equally well as a muffin, with or without the frosting.

INGREDIENTS

- 3 cups flour
- 2 teaspoons baking powder
- 1 teaspoon baking soda
- 2 teaspoons cinnamon
- ¼ teaspoon ground nutmeg
- ⅛ teaspoon ground cloves
- ⅛ teaspoon allspice
- 1 teaspoon salt
- 2 cups unrefined cane sugar
- 1 cup avocado oil
- 1 cup carrot puree*1
- ⅓ cup Vegan Egg
- 3 cups carrots, shredded
- 1 recipe Cream Cheese Frosting (recipe follows below)

OPTIONAL: shredded coconut or chopped nuts

PROCEDURES

Preheat oven to 350°F.

Prepare two 8" round cake tins by greasing the bottom and sides with butter and sprinkling flour to coat. Shake off excess flour. Line both cake pans with parchment rounds.

Mix dry ingredients together: flour, baking powder, baking soda, cinnamon, nutmeg, cloves, allspice, and salt.

In large bowl, beat wet ingredients until well blended, at least 2 minutes: sugar, oil, carrot puree, and Vegan Egg.

Add the carrots.

Add the dry ingredients in 3 steps, just until blended.

Pour the batter equally into the two cake pans.

Bake 30-35 minutes or until a toothpick comes out clean in the center.

Allow the layers to cool for 10-15 minutes in their pans on a wire rack; then release them from the pans, remove the parchment papers, turn them right-side up, and allow to cool completely before assembling the cake.

To assemble the cake, put a dollop of the frosting in the center of the cake plate. This will help the bottom cake layer to adhere to the cake plate.

Place one layer, top side down, onto the plate. If the layer rose in the center, use a serrated-edge knife to level it off.

Spread some frosting on the top of the cake layer.

Place the second cake layer, right-side up, on top of the 1st frosted layer.

Frost the outside of the cake, starting with the top, then the side.

Optional, you can press shredded coconut or chopped nuts, or a mixture of both, onto the side of the cake.

Refrigerate at least 1-2 hours to set before serving.

*1 To make carrot puree, blend shredded carrots with a scant amount of water. If the mixture is too thick, add a small amount of water until you have a puree similar to the consistency of baby food. If you don't want to use carrot puree, you can swap it out for apple sauce, but it will dilute the carrot flavor.

NOTE: These cake layers, if wrapped and sealed tightly, freeze incredibly well.

CREAM CHEESE FROSTING

INGREDIENTS

- ¼ cup butter, softened to room temperature
- 1 8-ounce container cream cheese, softened to room temperature
- 3-5 cups sifted powdered sugar & tapioca/rice flour, in equal parts*1

PROCEDURES

In a large mixing bowl with a hand mixer or using a stand mixer, combine all the ingredients until light and fluffy.

*1 I, personally, am not a fan of cloying sweet frostings, which is why I use equal parts powdered sugar and tapioca/rice flour. If you prefer you can certainly feel free to up the amount of powdered sugar as you reduce the tapioca/rice flour.

CHAPTER 10

FOR THE SWEET TOOTH

DESSERTS FOR ALL OCCASIONS – OR JUST BECAUSE, EVEN BETTER

Baker or not, you will find these recipes approachable and easy to create in the comfort of your own kitchen. Watch and enjoy as they are quickly devoured, bringing delight to all.

POACHED PEARS WITH MERINGUE AND CHOCOLATE DRIZZLE

This is the perfect dessert for entertaining because all the components are prepared in advance with only the dessert assembly done just before serving. It's impressive, easy, and outstandingly enchanting.

THE PEARS

INGREDIENTS

- 6 firm pears
- 1 bottle Merlot or Shiraz
- 1 cinnamon stick
- 4 cloves, whole
- 2 allspice berries, gently cracked

PROCEDURES

In a large stock pot, add the wine and spices. Bring to a gentle simmer to scent the wine. Set aside to cool. Use a pot that will enable the wine to completely cover the pears.

Prepare the pears. Using a small spoon or corer, remove the seeds from the pear from the bottom of the pear. Peel the skin but leave the stem intact.

Add the pears to the wine. Bring the liquid to a gentle simmer, cover the pot, and poach the pears for 15-20 minutes, or until barely fork tender. Do not overcook. Remove from the heat and allow the pears to cool in the wine mixture. The pears will continue to cook during the cooling process, so be sure to not overcook.

Remove pears. If serving shortly, you can allow them to come to room temperature. If not, park in the refrigerator; but bring them to room temperature just before serving.

THE MERINGUE COOKIES

INGREDIENTS

- Aquafaba from one 15-ounce can of garbanzo beans, at room temperature
- 1 teaspoon cream of tartar
- ⅔ cup unrefined sugar, processed to a smaller grain
- 2 teaspoons extract (vanilla, almond, coconut, etc.)

PROCEDURES

Preheat oven to 250°F.

Line a cookie sheet with parchment paper.

Using a stand mixer with the whisk attachment, pour the aquafaba into the bowl and begin whipping the aquafaba at low speed, increasing to high speed.

Continue beating until soft peaks begin to form. This should take 12-15 minutes.

Add in the cream of tartar and continue whipping.

Slowly add the sugar until all combined.

Whisk in the extract.

Using either a tablespoon, a small melon scoop, or a pastry bag with a wide enough tip to extrude the whipped aquafaba, scoop the meringue onto the parchment-lined cookie sheet(s).

Bake for 1½ – 2 hours, until meringues are dried out and crispy on the outside.

Remove from oven and allow to cool on the cookie sheet on a wire rack until they are dry and firm.

Meringues will last in a tightly-sealed container for 2-3 days. If they begin to get a little soggy, you can refresh them by repeating the baking process for approximately 15-20 minutes.

THE CHOCOLATE DRIZZLE

INGREDIENTS

- 1 3.5-ounce bar of dark chocolate
- 3 tablespoons milk
- Optional: 1 tablespoon Liqueur, such as Kalhua, Gran Marnier, Cherry Liqueur

PROCEDURES

In a double boiler, combine the chocolate and milk (and liqueur, if using) over gently simmering water until chocolate is melted and mixture becomes smooth and glistening. Whisk to combine; but gently so as not to incorporate air bubbles.

Remove from heat, allow to cool, and then pour into a squeeze bottle.

If you are going to park this, you can refrigerate it, then bring it back to its viscous syrup in the double boiler, repeating the cooling and pouring into the squeeze bottle.

ASSEMBLING DESSERT

Cut the pears in half lengthwise. Arrange the pear on a dessert plate with cut sides facing up.

Place a meringue cookie on the round part of the pear.

Drizzle the pear and meringue with the chocolate sauce.

OR, you can stand up the whole pear, drizzle with the chocolate, and place the meringue cookie offset on the plate.

Serve immediately.

OPTIONS

Make Pears En Croute, another easy and impressive dessert. After you poach and cool the pears, you can wrap them in either several layers of phyllo dough prepped by coating each layer with butter, or you can also use sheets of puff pastry (Pepperidge Farm Puff Pastry is vegan).

To bring this to yet another level, you can stuff the hole created from coring the pears with chopped nuts.

Bake at 400°F for approximately 25 minutes, or until the pastry is golden and cooked through. The pears are already cooked, so you just want to ensure that they pastry is cooked through. Serve warm or at room temperature with a scoop of ice cream and a chocolate drizzle.

"I AM NOT A CROOK" WATERGATE SALAD

A tribute to our 37th President, Richard Milhous Nixon, in the form of a popular 1970's salad – I give you, The Watergate Salad. A riff on the 1960's classic, Ambrosia Salad, this salad boasts of pineapple and pistachios.

INGREDIENTS

- ¼ cup sugar
- ⅓ cup powdered coconut milk
- ¼ teaspoon sea salt
- 2 tablespoons ground pistachios (ground to a powder)
- 1 20-ounce can crushed pineapple in juice, drained and separated
- 1 cup miniature marshmallows
- ⅔ cup chopped pistachios
- 2 teaspoons pistachio extract
- 1½ cups Frozen Whipped Topping, defrosted

PROCEDURES

In a large mixing bowl, whisk together the sugar, powdered milk, salt, and pistachio powder until well combined.

Add the pineapple juice, and whisk until combined and smooth.

Gently mix in the crushed pineapple, marshmallows, chopped pistachios, and pistachio extract until well combined.

Fold in the defrosted whipped topping.

Refrigerate the salad for at least 1 hour before serving.

Serve in individual dessert cups.

OPTIONAL

Sprinkle with additional chopped pistachios.

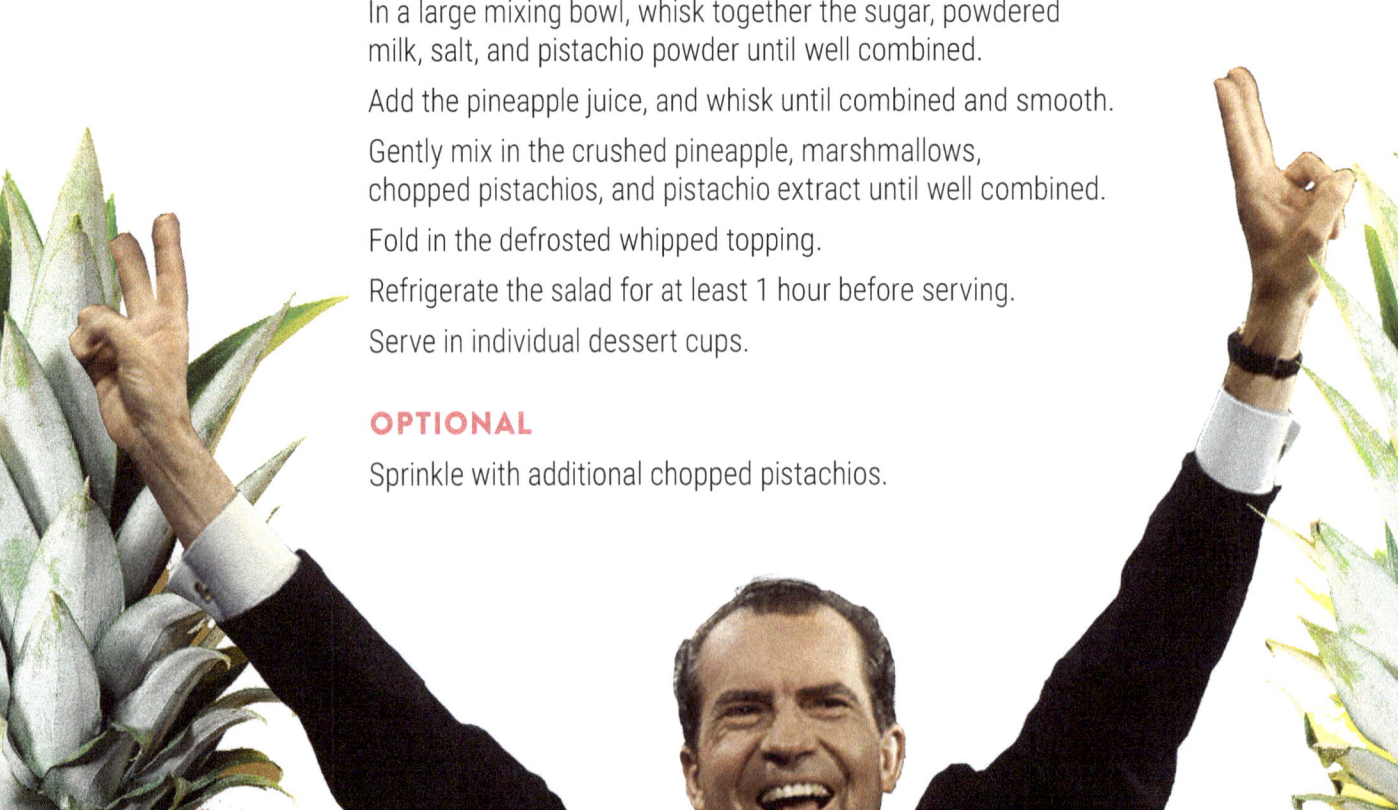

BLOOD ORANGE TAHINI CAKE

While this cake is definitely blood-orange forward, the back-note of the tahini brings a welcome complexity and moistness to this cake, which has no added oil.

INGREDIENTS

- 3-4 blood oranges
- 1½ cups plus 2 tablespoons white whole wheat pastry flour
- 1 tablespoon corn starch, tapioca or rice flour, or arrowroot
- ¾ teaspoon baking soda
- ⅓ teaspoon sea salt
- 1 cup sugar
- ¼ cup tahini
- 1 teaspoon white cider vinegar or champagne vinegar
- 1 teaspoon vanilla extract

PROCEDURES

Preheat oven to 350°F.

Grease and lightly dust a 9"x5" loaf pan. Set aside.

Zest the blood oranges and set zest aside.

Juice the oranges. You will need 1 cup of blood orange juice. Set aside.

In a medium-sized bowl whisk together your dry ingredients: flour, starch, baking soda, sea salt. Set aside.

In a large mixing bowl or stand mixer, mix the wet ingredients until well combined: juice from the orange, sugar, tahini vinegar, vanilla. Add the zest.

Add the dry ingredients to the bowl and mix until batter is well combined and smooth.

Pour the batter into the prepared loaf pan.

Bake for 30-35 minutes, or until a toothpick comes out clean in the center of the cake.

Remove from oven, and cool for 10 minutes in the pan on a wire rack before removing cake from the pan.

Allow cake to cool completely before serving.

SERVING SUGGESTIONS

Dollop with coconut whipped cream and blood orange segments that you've supremed*1.

Glaze the cake: combine 3 tablespoons blood orange juice with ⅓ cup of confectioner's sugar until smooth. Drizzle over cake. If you want a spiked glaze, swap out the blood orange juice with Gran Marnier.

Another glaze idea: In a small saucepan, combine ¼-⅓ cup orange marmalade with 1 tablespoon of Gran Marnier until the mixture is smooth and viscous. Allow to cool slightly, then drizzle over the cake.

*1 How to supreme any kind or citrus fruit: Cut off a small section of both the top and bottom or the fruit.

Using a paring knife and following the curve of the fruit, peel the sides being careful to remove all the white pith.

Holding the fruit in your non-dominant hand over a bowl (so that you catch all the juice in this process), and with the paring knife in your dominant hand, carefully and gently cut slices between each membrane, which will then release the fruit segments into the bowl.

When you are finished supreming the fruit, squeeze the remaining fruit into the bowl to capture all the juice from the fruit.

BLACK BEAN BROWNIES

Yes, BLACK BEAN brownies. It's the black beans that make these brownies not only moist but more importantly, no one will ever guess that you used a legume to attain that fudgy interior with a slightly crisp crackle-top. Make a double batch. These will go quickly. And they freeze incredibly well. As an option, I love topping these with a ganache that reminds me of when I was a child, taking those brand-name frozen brownies with the chocolate frosting out the freezer and not waiting for them to defrost before devouring them.

INGREDIENTS

- 1½ cups whole wheat flour
- 2¼ cups raw sugar
- 1¼ cup raw cocao powder
- 4 teaspoons instant coffee powder
- 1 teaspoon salt
- 1 teaspoon baking powder
- 1 15-ounce can black beans, rinsed and filled with new water
- 1 cup of water
- 1 tsp vanilla
- 1½ cups chopped nuts, optional (walnuts or pecans are my personal favorites)

GANACHE

Optional, but highly recommended

- 6 ounces dark chocolate, at least 70% cacao
- ¾ cup vanilla or hazelnut coffee creamer
- 1 teaspoon instant espresso
- ½ teaspoon sea salt

PROCEDURES

Preheat the oven to 350°F.

Grease a 9"x13" pan.

In a large mixing bowl, whisk together all the dry ingredients: flour, sugar, cocoa powder, instant coffee, salt, and baking powder. Set aside.

Drain a can of black beans and rinse thoroughly until the water runs clear. Return the black beans back to the can, and then fill the rest of the can to the top with water.

Put the beans and water into a food processor and puree.

Add the puree to the dry mix along with the one cup of water and vanilla. Stir to combine, but do not over-mix. You want the batter to be just combined.

Gently fold in the nuts, if using.

Pour the batter into the prepared baking pan and bake for 25-30 minutes. Rotate the pan halfway through the baking process.

You will know that the brownies are done because they will be firm in the center and the edges will be slightly puffy and starting to pull away from the sides.

IMPORTANT NOTE: Do not over bake in the oven because of the carry-over baking once out of the oven. If you over bake them in the oven, they will be dry once cooled.

Let the brownies cool completely in the pan on a wire rack.

To make the ganache, add the chocolate, coffee creamer, espresso powder, and salt into a bowl, and place on top of a pot with 1" of water to create a double boiler.

Bring the water in the bottom pot to a low simmer. Be sure that the steam does not come out of the sides and that the water does not touch the bottom of the upper bowl.

When the chocolate appears to have melted, remove from the heat and gently stir to combine. Do not use a wire whisk as you do not want to aerate the ganache. You only want to combine the ingredients so that they become a silky homogeneous blend.

Remove from the heat and allow to cool.

Spread the ganache over the brownies, then slice into 24 squares.

PUMPKIN PECAN CHOCOLATE MAGIC BARS

Magic bars are a wonderful way to bring children into the kitchen. This is a fun and easy recipe to put together with ingredients you might typically have in your pantry. The fragrant pumpkin filling, coupled with the chocolate ganache topping and clotted cream, is simply intoxicating.

CRUST
- 3 cups pecans, raw
- 1 cup pitted Medjool dates, slightly packed
- ¾ cup raw cacao powder
- 3 teaspoons vanilla
- ½ teaspoon Himalayan sea salt

FILLING
- 2 cups pumpkin pureé
- ⅓ cup coconut milk
- 2 tablespoons Vegan Egg
- ¼ cup dark brown sugar
- ⅓ cup white whole wheat pastry flour
- 2-3 tablespoons unrefined cane sugar
- 1 tablespoon molasses
- 2 tablespoons finely minced crystallized ginger
- 1 teaspoon cinnamon
- ¼ teaspoon nutmeg
- ¼ teaspoon ground cloves
- ¼ teaspoon salt

TOPPING
- 1 recipe Chocolate Ganache
- 1 recipe Clotted Cream (See Page 28)
- ½ cup shredded coconut
- ½ cup chopped pecans

TO MAKE THE MAGIC BARS

Soak the pecans for two hours, then drain.

Preheat oven to 400°F.

Prepare a 9"x13" baking pan by spraying it with avocado oil.

In the large bowl of a food processor, process the pecans until finely minced.

Add the remaining crust ingredients, and continue to process until well blended.

Press the crust into the bottom of the pan, spreading evenly.

Using a stand mixer or portable hand mixer, combine all the filling ingredients until well blended.

Spread pumpkin filling on top of the crust.

Bake for ten minutes at 400°F; then reduce heat to 350°F (do not open oven door).

Bake for an additional 30-35 minutes, or until pumpkin filling is set.

Allow to cool completely and refrigerate for at least 2 hours before moving on to the next steps.

Spread ganache over pumpkin filling and refrigerate for 15-25 minutes.

Spread clotted cream over ganache.

Top with coconut and pecans, lightly pressing into the clotted cream.

Refrigerate for at least 2 hours before serving.

GANACHE

INGREDIENTS
- 10 ounces dark chocolate bar, chopped
- ½ cup coconut milk

PROCEDURES
Place chocolate in bowl.
In a saucepan, heat the coconut milk, but do not boil.
Pour the coconut milk into the chocolate and stir until homogeneous and glossy.
Set aside to cool.

RAW KEY LIME BARS

These delightful, raw bars are best served cold but not frozen; however, I have been known to keep them frozen and thaw until just able to cut for a refreshing summertime dessert.

CRUST
INGREDIENTS
- 1½ cup Walnuts
- 1 cup shredded coconut or coconut flakes
- 1 cup Medjool dates, pitted
- 1 teaspoon vanilla extract
- Splash of water
- Pinch of sea salt

KEY LIME CUSTARD
INGREDIENTS
- 2¼ cups raw cashews
- ½ cup Key lime juice
- ¼ cup maple syrup
- 2 tablespoons Lime Zest
- 2 teaspoons vanilla extract
- ⅓ cup coconut oil
- Shredded coconut or coconut flakes, for garnish

PROCEDURES

The night before you intend to make your key lime bars, place cashews in a bowl of water and let soak overnight.

Add walnuts, coconut, dates, vanilla extract, water and salt to a food processor or blender and pulse until sticky mounds begin to form.

Press the crust into an 8x8 freezer-safe pan lined with parchment paper with the ends hanging over the sides, which will aid in removing the bars from the pan.

Drain the cashews well and add to the food processor. Blend until smooth.

Scrape down the sides of the processor and add lime juice, maple syrup, lime zest, and vanilla extract.

Blend until smooth, adding the coconut oil half way through the blending process.

Spread the mixture on top of your crust and garnish with more lime zest and coconut.

Cover with foil and freeze for 3 hours or until set. This time-frame will set the pie but not make it frozen solid. You can certainly freeze it for use at a later date and either thaw in the refrigerator or leave out for 10-15 minutes and slice, so that you have a frozen dessert, somewhat akin to a semifreddo.

GRANDMA MARY'S PIGNOLI COOKIES

Don't you just love being resourceful? Whoever had the brilliant idea of using the liquid from a can of garbanzo beans as an egg white rather than tossing it down the kitchen drain is nothing short of a culinary genius! Oh, and the name it's been given – Aquafaba – now how's that for a fancy-shmanzy term. (Actually, it was Joel Roessel, a French chef, in 2014, and furthered by the United States' own Goose Wohlt, in 2015, who gave this liquid its rather gastronomic name, "Aquafaba.) I don't know about you, but I love it! And I love Aquafaba. I am a believer.

"But, What to do with it, what to do with it?" was the question when I first came upon the notion that a bean liquid could double as an egg white. Ah, but of course! My Grandma Mary's Pignoli Cookies.

Also, however, there was a problem beyond not knowing how the aquafaba would work in place of egg whites. When I put my fingers on her passed-down recipe, I not only needed to tweak it to accommodate the swapping out of the aquafaba for the egg whites (and her recipe also called for honey, but that's an easy swap), I also did not have any of the other ingredients in my pantry, specifically no almond paste, a key ingredient second only to the egg whites. So, this meant I really needed to virtually write an entirely new recipe.

I rolled up my sleeves, and got to work. Here's what I came up with ...

INGREDIENTS

- Aquafaba from one 15-ounce can of garbanzo beans, refrigerated until chilled*1
- ½ teaspoon cream of tartar
- 2½ cups confectioner's sugar
- 4 tablespoons agave
- ½ teaspoon salt
- 3 cups super-fine almond flour
- 1 cup Pine Nuts

*1 It should measure out to approximately ⅔ cup liquid.

*2 When I'm teaching a class that involves whipping aquafaba to the point of stiff peaks, this is the time when I break out and have a little fun. I ask the class, "how do you know when your aquafaba has formed stiff peaks?" I proceed to remove the bowl from the stand and turn the bowl upside down. Lo and behold, the aquafaba remains in the bowl. There's always at least one gasp from the participants as I'm turning over the bowl. Such fun.

PROCEDURES

Preheat oven to 350°F. Prepare three cookies sheets by lining them with parchment paper. Set aside.

Pour the chilled aquafaba into a large electric mixer bowl. Turn on high and beat until soft peaks begin to form. It should take approximately 2-3 minutes.

Add the cream of tartar and beat for an additional 2 minutes.

Add the confectioner's sugar, and beat for an additional 10 minutes. Stiff peaks will form.*2

While the mixer is continuing to beat, slowly add in the agave, and salt. Continue beating until the soft white peaks glisten. This step should take approximately 2-3 minutes.

Add the almond flour and beat until mixture is light and fluffy, with soft peaks remaining.

With a large piping tip in a pastry bag, open the lip of the bag wide, folding the top ⅓ over to the outside. Fill the pastry bag with the batter. The batter will be sticky, so to facilitate this step, put the bag inside a tall vase that you can fold the top ⅓ of the bag over the edge to steady the bag. Once filled, fold the top over.

Guiding the pastry bag, pipe 1½-inch rounds about 1½ inches apart. Top each cookie with at least one dozen pignoli nuts.

Refrigerate the pan of cookies for 15-20 minutes before placing in oven. This step is critical as it will help reduce the spreading in the oven.

Bake the cookies for 13-16 minutes, until just golden brown around the edges.

Remove from oven and slide cookies still on the parchment paper onto wire racks to cool.

Allow to cool completely, then peel the cookies off the parchment paper and place onto a wire rack to continue setting.

NOTE: These cookies will soften if left out and not served that day. If preparing for another day, you can line the cooled cookies on parchment paper-lined cookie sheet and freeze in the freezer. Once frozen, you can stack them in a freezer-safe airtight container until you are ready to use them. Before serving, line them on a cookie sheet lined with parchment paper and re-firm in a pre-heated 350°F oven for no more than 2 minutes, then repeating the cooling process as if they were freshly baked. Stack on a lovely cookie platter, and your cookies will be an absolute delight!

COCONUT CHOCOLATE-DIPPED COOKIES

These easy-to-create cookies will be the hit of any dessert table.

INGREDIENTS

- ¾ cup unsweetened shredded coconut
- ¾ cup unsweetened coconut flakes
- 1 cup white whole wheat flour
- 1 teaspoon baking powder
- ½ teaspoon salt
- ¼ cup coconut sugar
- ⅓ cup coconut nectar or light agave syrup
- ¼ cup plus 1 tablespoon coconut oil, separated*1
- 10 ounce bag chocolate chips or dark chocolate bar

PROCEDURES

Preheat oven to 350 degrees.

Line a large baking sheet with parchment paper.

In a dry skillet over medium heat, add coconut and stir constantly until flakes are golden brown. Toast the shredded coconut and coconut flakes separately as the shredded coconut will toast more quickly than the flakes. Set aside in a large bowl, and allow to cool completely.

Once coconut has cooled, whisk in flour, baking powder, and salt.

In a large bowl using a hand mixer or stand mixer, combine sugar, nectar/agave syrup, and ¼ cup coconut oil. Mix well.

Add wet mixture into the dry mixture. Mix until just combined, being careful not to over-beat.

Using a 3-ounce ice cream scoop, you should get ten (10) rounds of cookie dough. Place them on the parchment-lined cookie sheet at least 1½ inches apart.*2

With wet fingers, press cookie rounds down slightly to even the tops as they will not spread out much while baking.*3

Bake for 10 to 12 minutes, until barely browned around the edges and no longer shiny on top.

Let cookies rest on the baking sheet for 10 minutes before transferring to a wire rack to cool completely.

In a double boiler, melt the chocolate and the remaining 1 tablespoon coconut oil. Dip the bottoms of the cookies in the melted chocolate and set on a parchment-line cookie sheet and refrigerate 10 to 15 minutes to allow the chocolate to set. (You could also dip half the cookie in the chocolate sideways to give the cookie a black-and-white cookie effect.)

*1 my preference, to keep with the coconut theme or butter, melted

*2 If you want smaller cookies, use a rounded tablespoon, which will yield approximately 20 cookies.

*3 I keep a small finger bowl next to me so that I can dip my fingers into it before forming each cookie.

FRUIT CAKE COOKIES

This no-flour cookie, made with old-fashioned rolled oats, is packed with lots of macerated dried fruits, dark chocolate chips, and nut/seed butter. Perfect with a hot cup of tea or packed in your knapsack for your hiking energy-booster snack, these cookies are dense, hearty, and just outright yummy.

INGREDIENTS

- ½ cup raisins
- ½ cup dried blueberries
- ½ cup dried cranberries
- ¼ cup dried cherries
- ¼ cup bourbon
- 2 teaspoons baking soda
- 4½ cups old-fashioned rolled oats (not instant)
- 1 cup coconut sugar
- ⅓ cup date syrup, brown rice syrup, or agave
- ⅓ cup organic unrefined cane sugar
- 4½ teaspoons vegan egg substitute powder mixed with enough water to make a loose paste, or ¼ cup JUST Egg
- ½ teaspoon salt
- 1 teaspoon vanilla extract
- 1 12-ounce jar organic unsweetened peanut butter or nut/seed butter with no added oils or salt
- 3 ounces butter
- ¾ cup chocolate chips
- Water, as needed, in a finger bowl

PROCEDURES

Preheat oven to 340° Fahrenheit.

Line three large cookie sheets with parchment paper.

In a bowl, toss the raisins, blueberries, cranberries, and cherries with the bourbon. Stir and set aside. Allow the fruits to macerate for at least ½ hour, tossing frequently. Drain, then gently pat dry. Set aside.

In a bowl, whisk the oatmeal with the baking soda. Set aside.

In a very large mixing bowl, combine the coconut sugar, date syrup, cane sugar, and egg substitute. Using a stand mixer or an electric hand mixer helps to readily emulsify the ingredients.

Add the salt, vanilla, peanut butter, and butter. Blend in the mixer until well combined.

Using a wooden spoon (or my personal favorite, my hands), stir in the chocolate chips, raisins, blueberries, cranberries, and cherries. Mix until well combined.

Dump the oatmeal into the bowl.

Using the wooden spoon or your hands, mix to combine evenly. If the mixture feels too dry, you can add a tablespoon of water at a time. You want a sticky mixture, not dry but also not wet. It will be crumbly, but if you press some of it together in the palm of your hand, it will stick together.

Using a standard size ice cream scoop[*1], gently press the dough into the scoop, then drop on the lined cookie sheet. Repeat until you have all the dough scooped out onto the cookie sheet, allowing 3" between each mound.

Using damp, not wet, fingers (have a finger bowl of water next to you), use one hand to keep the cookie round as you press down flatly with your other hand. This will ensure a compact cookie that is beautifully round.

Continue until you have all the cookies formed on your sheets.

Refrigerate each pan for at least 15 minutes before placing them in the oven, baking one pan at a time.

Bake for 15 minutes.

Do not overbake.

Take the tray out of the oven, and set the tray on a wire rack for 5-8 minutes, then slide the cookies still on the parchment paper out of the pan and onto the wire rack.

Allow the cookies to cool on the parchment paper on the wire rack for an additional 10-12 minutes, then remove from the parchment paper.

Allow the cookies to cool completely.

NOTE: This is my holiday version. Throughout the year, I swap out the macerated fruits and add nuts, coconut, vegan white chocolate chips or vegan M&M's, and dried but not macerated fruit. Create your own version with add-ins of your choice just making sure that you stick with the same total volume of ingredients.

NOTE: These cookies freeze exceptionally well, so always make more for later.

[*1] You can really use any size you want depending on the cookie size you are looking for, but you will need to adjust the baking time accordingly.

STRUFFOLI

My Grandma Mary only made these cookies during the Christmas Holiday season. Typically soaked in honey, ours will have the honey swapped out for agave. She would stack hers on paper plates into the shape of a tree, which gave us kids the promise of Santa Claus, Christmas morning, and presents yet to come. Of course, being soaked in honey, by the time we got to them, the plate would be soaked and sticky, and as we got to the bottom of the plate, we typically also got a piece or two of paper plate with those last few bites of struffoli. Ah, we were kids, so it didn't matter much, if at all, to us then. Today, I don't use paper plates, hence instead, stack them on a pretty holiday platter.

INGREDIENTS

- 2⅔ cups white whole wheat pastry flour
- ¾ teaspoon baking powder
- ¼ teaspoon salt
- 5¾ tablespoons butter, melted
- 1 orange zested*1
- 2¾ tablespoons organic unrefined cane sugar
- 3 tablespoons Grand Marnier or orange juice
- ⅓ cup powdered vegan egg mixed with ½ cup plus 2 tablespoons water
- 10 ounces vegan 'honey', agave, or date syrup
- Avocado oil for frying – enough to bring the oil to 2-3" tall in a medium pot with high sides.
- Rainbow Candy Sprinkles
- Slivered almonds

PROCEDURES

In a large mixing bowl, whisk together the flour, baking powder, and salt.

In a smaller bowl, whisk together the melted butter, orange zest, sugar and Grand Marnier together.

Pour the wet ingredients into the dry ingredients.

Using a fork or pastry cutter, begin to combine the ingredients until crumbly.

Using an electric or hand mixer, add one-third of the vegan egg mixture until combined, then repeat process for the other two-thirds, one-third at a time.

When the dough is almost combined, put the dough on a lightly-flour surface. Knead, and if needed, you can add up to 1½ tablespoons flour if the dough is too wet. You want it to form a soft dough.

Cover the dough with a clean towel and let it rest for 30 minutes.

On a clean, lightly floured surface, roll out the dough into thin ropes that are approximately ¼" diameter.

Cut each rope into pieces the size of slightly smaller than a marble. You want to get all the pieces as close in size as possible.

Roll each piece into a ball.

Pour 2-3" of fresh avocado oil into a medium-sized pan with high sides. Preheat the oil to 350°F. You can use a candy thermometer; however, if you don't have one, carefully drop a ball into the oil. If the oil is hot enough, the oil around it will immediately begin to sizzle.

When the oil is up to temperature, fry the struffoli in small batches to avoid dropping the oil temperature and/or causing the oil to boil up and over the pot.

As they are frying, turn them to ensure they are evenly cooked. When they are golden brown, remove them from the oil and place on a paper-towel-lined cookie sheet to drain and cool. Repeat process until you have all the struffoli fried. You do not want to overcook the struffoli as they will then become hard. I used a spider for this step, which not only helps to move them about but also facilitates removing them when they are done.

Warm your 'honey' alternative in a pot until just lukewarm.

Put the cooled struffoli in a large mixing bowl.

Pour the 'honey' over them, stirring carefully to mix the 'honey' evenly without breaking the struffoli balls. You want the balls to be sticky but not dripping with 'honey'.

Stir in sprinkles and slivered almonds.

Shape into your desired form and sprinkle with more sprinkles and almonds. (You might want to very lightly oil the bottom of the plate to avoid sticking.)

NOTE: common shapes are stacked like a tree or a pyramid, and sort of a bundt-cake shape in that you pile up the struffoli balls in a circle, leaving a hole in the center.

*1 You'll be using only the zest, so go ahead and enjoy the orange ... baker's treat!

PIZZELLES

These Italian waffle cookies sprinkled with a touch of powdered sugar were always a staple in our house. Quick, easy, and fun to make in a pizzelle machine, you might want to make a double batch because they are irresistible. By varying up the flavorings, you can completely change the flavors. A versatile recipe, it is not just a waffle cookie. Use a pizzelle roller to make mini ice cream cones that you can fill with not only ice cream but how about a flavored pastry cream. Use a cannoli form and you have your own homemade cannoli shells ready to be filled with cannoli cream or a chocolate hazelnut mousse. I've made these sugar-free as well as gluten-free with outstanding results.

INGREDIENTS

- 4 cups white whole wheat pastry flour
- 2 teaspoons baking soda
- ¾ cup coconut milk (from the can, full-fat)
- 3 tablespoons egg replacer powder
- 12 ounces butter
- 1⅓ cup organic unrefined cane sugar or organic erythritol
- 4 teaspoons vanilla
- ½ cup confectioner's sugar

PROCEDURES

Preheat your pizzelle machine.

In a small bowl, sift the flour and baking soda together. Set aside.

Using a wire whisk, whisk the coconut milk and Egg Replacer together. Set aside.

In a large mixing bowl, whip together the butter, sugar, and vanilla until smooth and creamy.

Whip milk/egg replacer mixture into the butter/sugar mixture until well blended.

Gradually add flour mixture into wet mixture in 3-4 batches, mixing until blended.

Put 1 well-rounded teaspoon of batter onto pizzelle machine. Close lid and cook for 1 to 1¼ minutes, or golden.

Please cookies on a wire rack to cool.*1

When cooled, sprinkle with confectioner's sugar and stack in an airtight container.

VARIATIONS:
In place of vanilla, try adding one of these flavors: anise, licorice, almond, lemon, or coconut. Be creative. Drizzle with melted chocolate. Or, swap out some of the flour for cocao powder for a chocolate pizzelle. Add a mint extract for a chocolate peppermint pizzelle.

*1 Or, while still hot and straight off the griddle, use one of the forms to create cones or shells.

NEVER-FAIL BUTTERCREAM

There's nothing more delightful than a moist cake covered in a flavorful buttercream. But, I have to admit, that most often, it is far too cloyingly sweet for my tastes. So here's a version that I find creates that balance between sweet and flavorful yet doesn't overpower the tastebuds so that all you taste is sugary-sweetness. You can play with the ratio of powdered sugar to the tapioca/rice flour to suite your personal preference of sweetness.

INGREDIENTS

- ½ pound butter
- 2 cups powdered sugar
- 1½ cups tapioca or rice flour
- 2 tablespoons plus 1 teaspoon milk or water
- 2 teaspoons vanilla extract
- Pinch salt

PROCEDURES

Using electric hand or stand mixer, whip butter, powdered sugar and tapioca/rice flour until light and fluffy.

Add the milk or water, vanilla extract, and salt. Continue whipping until the frosting is smooth and creamy.

Refrigerate for at least ½ hour, or until somewhat firmer yet still creamy, before assembling cake.

NOTE

By swapping out some of the ingredients, you can create a completely different buttercream, frosting or icing. Here's a couple of ideas to get you thinking …

HARVEY WALLBANGER BUTTERCREAM

- Swap out the milk or water and vanilla extract for:
- 1 tablespoon plus 1 teaspoon Galliano Liqueur
- 1 tablespoon plus 1 teaspoon orange juice
- 1 teaspoon vodka

CREAM CHEESE FROSTING

- Swap out the butter for ½ pound full-fat cream cheese

MOCHA FROSTING

- Swap out ¼ cup powdered sugar for raw cacao. Add 2 teaspoons espresso powder, and 2 tablespoons melted chocolate, cooled.

INDEX, GLOSSARY & RESOURCES

Voorhis' Vegan Versions

LIST OF MY FAVORITE VEGAN VERSIONS OF TYPICALLY NON-VEGAN ITEMS

FOOD ITEM	BRAND/PRODUCT
Beer, Ale, Stout	Founder's Canadian Breakfast Stout
	Guinness Stout
Broth	Better Than Bouillon Vegetarian No Beef Base
	Better Than Bouillon Vegetarian No Chicken Base
Butter	Miyoko's Cultured Butter
	Forager Organic Dairy-Free Buttery Spread
Cheese	
Cheese	Violife - *Every one of their products rocks my world.*
	Rind by Dina & Joshua - *All their French-style, soft-ripened, and Bleu Cheese*
Cheese Slices	Field Roast Chao Cheese: Creamy Original and Tomato Cayenne
	Follow Your Heart Smoked Gouda
Cream Cheese	Kite Hill Original Almond Milk Cream Cheese
	Miyoko's Classic Double Cream Chive
Grated Parmesan	Follow Your Heart Parmesan Cheese
	Violife Just Life Parmesan Wedge
Mozzarella	Miyoko's Fresh Vegan Mozzarella
Ricotta	Kite Hill Ricotta
Chocolate	
Chocolate Bar for Eating & Baking	Cocoa Parlor Simple Pleasure 67 Roasted Hazelnuts & Pink Sea Salt
	Trader Joe's Pound Plus Dark Chocolate
Dark Chocolate	Trader Joe's Bulk Bar
Mexican	Taza Chocolate Organic Chocolate Mexicano Disc Cacao Puro
Coffee Alternatives	Coffig
Creamers	Ripple Foods Original Half and Half
Croissants	L'Artisane Creative Bakery by Carolina Molea
Egg Roll Wrappers	Nasoya Vegan Egg Roll Wraps
Egg Substitute	Follow Your Heart Vegan Egg
	Just Egg

Ice Cream	Haagen Dazs Peanut Butter Chocolate Fudge Non-Dairy Bar Van Leeuwen Brand - Any Vegan Flavor Chloe's Oat Milk Salted Caramel Pops
Mayonnaise	JUST Mayo
Meat Alternatives	Beyond Meat Italian Sausage Butler Soy Curls Field Roast Frankfurters Field Roast Breakfast Sausage Beyond Meat Breakfast Sausage Gardein The Ultimate Beefless Ground Crumbles Beyond Meat Beyond Burgers Beyond Meat Ground Meat Field Roast deli slices - all flavors
Namu Shoyu	Ohsawa Nama Shoyu, Organic
Non-Dairy Milks	Westsoy Organic Unsweetened Soy Milk Califia Farms Unsweetened Almond Milk Pacific Foods Organic Almond Non-Dairy Beverage Califa Farms Oatmillk Native Organic Coconut Milk
Phyllo Dough Sheets	The Fillo Factory Organic Fillo Dough
Puff Pastry	Pepperidge Farm Frozen Puff Pastry
Rice Paper Wrappers	Star Anise Foods Gluten Free Rice Paper Wrappers for Spring Rolls, Egg Roll Wrappers, Wonton Wrappers
Sour Cream	Good Karma Sour Cream
Sugar, Date	Now Foods Date Sugar
Sugar, Organic Cane	Wholesome Organic Sugar
Sweetened Condensed Milk	Nature's Charm Condensed Coconut Milk
Tofu	Wildwood Organic Extra-Firm Sprouted Soybean Tofu
Yogurt	Coyo Dairy Free Natural Organic Coconut Yogurt Forager Unsweetened Plain Dairy-Free Cashew Yogurt

APPS TO LOOK UP BEER, WINE, AND LIQUOR

Green Vegan

Barnivore

GLOSSARY

Agar Agar - is a red algae made from seaweed. It becomes jelly-like when mixed with a hot liquid. Used as a vegan gelatin.

Aquafaba - is the liquid from beans, typically garbanzo beans, that is used as an egg-white replacer.

Baking Powder - is used for leaving in baked goods; and is a mixture of sodium bicarbonate (baking soda) and cream of tartar. It requires not only a liquid and acidic ingredient but also heat for complete activation.

Baking Soda - is used for leaving in baked goods. It requires liquid and an acidic ingredient to activate the leavening process.

Bench Flour - is the flour that is used to dust your clean work surface so that the dough will not stick when you're kneading it.

Berbere - is an Ethiopian spice blend that includes chilis, garlic, fenugreek, allspice, coriander, and cardamom. Blends might also include cinnamon, ginger, black pepper, onion powder, paprika, and nutmeg.

Black Truffle Sea Salt - is sea salt which has flecks of dried black truffles or powder mixed in with the salt.

Blooming or Proofing Yeast - is the process of stirring dry yeast into a small amount of water, sometimes adding a touch of sugar. If the yeast is alive, the surface of the water will become bubbly or frothy. That is when you know the yeast is also activated.

Cacao Powder - Unlike cocoa powder which has been fermented and roasted at high temperatures, cacao powder starts with the same beans, however, it is neither fermented nor roasted. I personally always use only cacao powder as I find it to bring out a more dense chocolate flavor.

Chat, or Chop, Masala - both are savory Indian spice blends, typically containing at least cumin, coriander, fennel, amchur powder (dried mango), kala namak, asafetida, ginger, mint, black pepper, and ajwain seeds (which are similar to a cross between fennel and cumin).

Chia Seeds - are tiny black seeds. When combined with a liquid, they tend to become gelatinous. They can be used to make jams or jellies as well as being added to smoothies, porridge, or even sprinkled on top of a salad.

Chinese Five Spice - a common Chinese spice blend containing cinnamon, fennel, cloves, star anise, and Szechuan peppercorns.

Clotted Cream - classically served as an accompaniment to scones during a British high tea, it is typically heavy cream that has been heated to between 170°-180°F for approximately 12 hours. This process causes the cream to reduce and thicken to the consistency that is similar to cream cheese. Our recipe is completely devoid of not only the heavy cream but also the extensive amount of time.

Cream of Tartar - is a white powdery substance that is actually the byproduct of wine making. It is added to egg whites or aquafaba as a stabilizer, helping to keep the aeration and volume when they are whipped.

Dock - is the process of pricking holes, typically using a fork, into a pie crust so that when it is baked, air can escape so that the crust doesn't bubble up, creating pockets in the baked pie crust.

Duxelle - is a mixture of finely chopped, or minced, mushrooms, onions, and shallots sautéed in butter with either thyme or parsley.

Epazote - is an aromatic herb that is found is Mexican cuisine. While, at least to me, it smells like old, dirty gasoline, it does wonders to beans when added during the cooking process.

Erythritol - is a zero-calorie sweetener that is an equal measure to sugar, making it an easy swap out without having to adjust the liquid to dry ratio.

Farro - is an ancient whole grain that looks similar to barley but has a nutty flavor.

Flaxseed - ground to a powder and mixed with water, it can be used as an egg replacement in many recipes.

Galangal - also known as Siamese ginger, it has a much stronger and sort of peppery flavor. It is commonly used in Thai cuisine.

Garam Masalsa - An Indian spice blend that typically contains cinnamon, coriander, cumin, cardamom, and mace.

Harissa - is a hot chili paste commonly used in Moroccan dishes. Several varieties of chilies are typically ground with garlic, caraway seeds, coriander seeds, and cumin in oil to make a rather viscous paste.

Herbs de Provence - a rather floral-forward spice blend common in French cuisine. It includes lavender, rosemary, fennel, savory, basil, marjoram, oregano, parsley, and tarragon.

Kala Namak - Indian black sea salt. It actually has more of a pink hue, not black. It has a high sulfur content, so in addition to acting as a salt, it also brings an egg-like flavor to whatever you add it to.

Kombu - is dried kelp. When added to both the soaking and cooking liquids for beans, it helps to remove the 'musicaltiy' that is often associated with eating beans and legumes.

Lemongrass - is a perennial grass that grows into thin stalks and commonly used in flavoring Thai foods, particularly broths with a coconut base.

Limoncello - is an Italian lemon liqueur predominant in the Southern Regions of Italy. It is typically served in a small shot glass as a sweet dessert cordial.

Liquid Smoke - is a liquid flavoring agent that is used to impart a smokey flavor that would otherwise come from smoking over a wood fire.

Mise-en-place - French for 'to put into place' or 'everything in its place'. It is the process of preparing and organizing all the ingredients, utensils, cooking vessels, etc. that are required for a recipe before cooking.

Miso - is a salty Japanese flavoring base typically made from fermented soy beans, rice, or other grains.

Molé - is a Mexican marinade or gravy that is made from a variety of chilies, tomatoes, spices, Mexican chocolate, peanuts, sometimes dried fruit, as well as a myriad of other additions. It is a dark, hearty, mildly spicy, and complex gravy.

Namu Shoyu - is a raw, unpasteurized Japanese soy sauce.

Nutritional Yeast - is a deactivated yeast that is typically sold in flakes or powder. It imparts a cheesy flavor and is a source of B-12.

Prosecco - is to Italy what Champagne is to France. Both bubbly, Champagne has to be made with grapes from the Champagne Region of France. Similarly, Prosecco must be made with grapes from specific regions around Prosecco, Italy, and must contain a certain percentage of those grapes.

Poolish - is a loose yeast starter dough that is made in advance so that it ferments, and is later used as a separate ingredient in bread making.

Ras El Hanout - an aromatic Moroccan spice blend that typically includes cinnamon, cayenne, anise, turmeric and coriander.

Roux - typically equal parts fat (butter or oil) and flour that is stirred together over medium heat. It is cooked to either a white, blonde, or brown color, depending on the depth of coloring and flavor you would like to attain. It is used as a thickener in sauces. Cooking the flour also removes that raw flavor of the flour.

Saffron - saffron threads come from the crocus sativas flower and yields three threads of saffron. It can have a subtle or pungent flavor, and imparts a subtle yellow color. Used in rices or stews.

Sambuca - is an Italian anise-flavored liqueur.

Sauté - is the frying of food in a small amount of oil in a sauté, or frying pan.

Seitan - is vital wheat gluten. Commonly used to make meat alternatives by adding broth or water and flavoring ingredients, then kneading and boiling or steaming.

Simple Syrup - equal parts sugar and water mixed together over low heat just until the sugar dissolves.

Sourdough Starter - is a fermented mixture of flour and water that develops its own wild yeast over time. Is used to make leavened baked goods without needing to add yeast.

Spritz - is a quick, scant amount of a liquid that is lightly sprayed.

Sumac Berries - from the sumac flower, it has a sour and acidic flavor, almost reminiscent of lemons.

Tagine - is a North African dish, similar to a stew, which is also named after the earthenware cooking vessel that it is cooked in.

Tahini - is ground, hulled sesame seeds, ground into a paste with a consistency similar to peanut butter.

Tempeh - typically made from fermented soy beans, but can also be made with grains. Cultured and fermented, the soy and/or grains bind together for form a firm block and has a nutty flavor.

Vegan - is a lifestyle that includes eating a 100% plant-based diet. It embraces the practice of Ahimsa, the respect for all living beings and the practice of non-violence. It also includes environmental sustainability as well as the avoidance of the use of any animal products.

Vermouth - is a fortified wine, flavored with botanicals. Not all vermouth is vegan.

Vital Wheat Gluten - is the flour-like substance that is left after washing wheat flour dough until all the starch is removed. It becomes elastic in texture, and is the main ingredient in seitan.

White Whole Wheat Pastry Flour - is a 100% whole wheat that is ground from soft white wheat. It has a much lower protein content that refined flour so it is a great choice for baking whole-grain items.

Za'Atar - a Middle-Eastern spice blend that typically contains toasted sesame seeds, thyme, cumin, coriande, sumac, and salt.

INDEX

A

Agar Agar 38, 87, 144
Agave 20, 47, 48, 50, 81, 104, 105, 135, 136, 137, 138
Almond Cream 58
Amuse-Bouche Stuffed Potato Boats 34
Apple 23, 58, 62, 65, 82, 126
Apple Cider Vinegar 48, 50, 66, 94
Apple Fennel Salad 62
Aquafaba 35, 38, 95, 128, 135, 144
Arugula 52, 62
Asparagus 21
Autumn Harvest Sauce 47
Avocado 38, 44, 57, 64, 120
Avocado Oil 20, 21, 24, 25, 26, 27, 34, 39, 44, 77, 78, 79, 81, 84, 85, 88,
         90, 99,104, 105, 106, 107, 108, 113, 116, 119, 124, 126, 133, 138
Award Winning Pumpkin Pecan Cranberry Muffins 25

B

Baked Stuffed French Toast 20
Bamboo Shoots 74, 79
Barbecue Sauce 90, 91
Beans
   Black Beans 57, 70, 88, 89, 132
   Cannellini Bean 53, 66
   Fava Beans 92
   Garbanzo Beans 35, 38, 40, 84, 95, 128, 135, 144
   Garbanzo (Chichi) 40, 41
Beatific Beet Burgers 99
Beef Wellington with Mushroom Spinach Stuffing and Brown Gravy 84
Berbere 96, 97, 144
Biscuits 30
Black Bean Brownies 132
Black Bean Soup 57
Black Truffle Sea Salt 36, 37, 144
Blender Hollandaise Sauce 44
Blood Orange 62, 131
Blood Orange Tahini Cake 131
Bolognese 45, 82, 100

Broccoli 28, 54, 56, 66, 113
Broccoli Rabe. 39
Brown Rice Syrup 55, 104, 137
Brussels Sprouts. 21, 65, 95
Buttercream Icing 117, 140
Buttermilk 20, 30, 62, 63
Buttermilk Biscuits With Country "Red-Eye" Mushroom Gravy 30
Buttermilk Ranch Dressing 63
Butternut Squash 47, 58, 75, 80, 95, 96
Butternut Squash Coconut Curry Stew with Tempeh 95
Butternut Squash Soup with Almond Cream & Spiced Pumpkin Seeds 58

C

Cabbage. 77, 79
Cacao Powder 120, 132,133, 140, 145
Cajun-Inspired Meatloaf 90
Carrot 45, 47, 66, 74, 79, 80, 92, 95, 96, 126
Carrot Cake with Cream Cheese Frosting 126
Cashew Crema 48, 88
Cauliflower. 56, 96
Cauliflower & Macaroni Soup 56
Chat Masala. 44
Cheesy Rapini Spiral Pastries 39
Cherry Orange Pecan Country Loaf 105
Chesapeake Bay Crabby Cakes. 93
Chia Seeds 29, 144
Chichi Bean Spread. 40
Chichi Bean Spread and Olive Tapenade On Crostini 40
Chilies
    Chipotle 57, 58
    Mulato Chilies 88
Chinese Egg-Less Roll 78
Chinese Five Spice 79, 144
Chop Masala 44, 144
Cilantro 37, 40, 41, 42, 48, 49, 50, 52, 55, 57, 70, 80, 88, 95
Clotted Cream 28, 133, 144
Coconut Chocolate Dipped Cookies. 136
Coconut 116, 126, 133, 134, 136, 137
    Coconut Cream. 89
    Coconut Custard. 107

    Coconut Milk 23, 27, 28, 29, 47, 55, 82, 89, 95, 106, 116, 120, 122, 130, 133, 139
    Coconut Nectar 136
    Coconut Oil 35, 78, 122, 134, 136
    Coconut Sugar 122, 136, 137
    Coconut Vinegar 59
    Coconut Yogurt 122
Coffee 31, 64, 88, 105, 120, 132
Coquilles St. Jacques À La Provencale 86
Corn 55, 68, 69, 70, 81
Corn Muffins 24
Country "Red-Eye" Mushroom Gravy 31
Cranberries 23, 25, 65, 122, 137
Cream Cheese Frosting 126, 140
Creamy-Dreamy Cannellini Bean Soup 53
Creamy Pasta Primavera Salad 66
Crème Anglaise 82
Crostini 40, 41
Crumbled Za'atar Tofu 64
Cucumber 52, 64

D

Dates 124, 133, 134
Dessert Bollo With Crème Anglaise 81
Devlish Eggs 38
Divinely-Decadent Chocolate Stout Cake 120
Dolmas 72

E

Egg 20, 23, 24, 25, 26, 27, 28, 38, 39, 44, 74, 78, 79, 82, 90, 93, 94, 97, 106, 108, 109, 119, 120, 122, 124, 126, 133, 135, 137, 138, 139
Eggplant 75, 92, 94
Eggplant and Rice Parmigiana 94
English Muffins 44, 99, 104
Epazote 88, 89, 144
Erythritol 139, 145
Espresso 27, 31, 38, 121, 132, 140
Ethiopian-Spiced Roasted Root Vegetable Tart 96

F

Farro	64, 145
Fennel	45, 62, 79, 92, 144
Flour	
Almond Flour	35, 135
Gluten-Free Flour	31, 86, 104, 122
Rice Flour	28, 117, 119, 126, 131, 140
Tapioca	28, 117, 126, 131, 140
White Whole Wheat Flour	104, 105, 122, 136
Focaccia	62, 63, 110, 111
Fruit Cake Cookies	137

G

Galangal	55, 145
Ganache	132, 133
Garlic	34, 35, 37, 39, 41, 42, 44, 45, 46, 47, 48, 49, 50, 53, 54, 55, 56, 57, 58, 59, 63, 65, 66, 68, 69, 70, 73, 75, 80, 85, 86, 87, 88, 94, 95, 97, 113, 144
Gazpacho	52
Ginger	20, 26, 42, 55, 74, 81, 95, 97, 124, 133, 144
Grandma Mary's Bread Loaf	108
Grandma Mary's Pignoli Cookies	135
Grape Leaves	72
Gremolata	59
Grilled Caesar Salad with Buttermilk Dill Dressing and Focaccia Crumble	62

H

Harissa	50, 65, 145
Hash Brown Waffles	22
Hearts Of Palm	93
Herbed Olive Oil	36, 37
Herbs De Provence	42, 145
Herbs De Provence Cashew Cheese Spread	42, 145
Horseradish	50, 93
Horseradish Sauce	50

I

"I Am Not A Crook" Watergate Salad	130
Indian Cilantro Chutney	50, 80
Indian Pistachio Date and Cardamom Cake	124
Italian Saffron Rice Torta	119

J

Jalapeño Pepper Poppers 37

K

Kala Namak 20, 21, 38, 84, 145
Kale 98
Key Lime 134
Kombu 88, 89, 145

L

Leeks 21, 53, 59, 96
Lemon 20, 28, 29, 30, 38, 44, 49, 50, 58, 59,
                63, 64, 65, 66, 70, 72, 75, 87, 92, 107, 109, 116, 118, 119, 139
Lemon-Chive Dressing 50
Lemon Curd 28
Lemongrass 42, 58, 95, 145
Lentils 90, 99
Lime 48, 49, 55, 70, 118, 134
Limoncello 116, 117, 118, 145
Limoncello Coconut Cake 116

M

Macaroni 56
Mango 29, 49, 88, 89
Mango Sticky Rice 89
Maple Butter 20, 29
Maple Harissa Dressing 50, 65
Maple Syrup 20, 29, 48, 50, 81, 104, 134
Meringue 35, 128, 129
Middle Eastern Farro Salad 64
Minestra di Verdura e Riso 54
Mini Roasted Red Pepper Quiche 35
Miso 75, 145
Molasses 118, 124, 133
Mole Black Bean Stew With Mango Sticky Rice 88
Muffin 24, 25, 26, 27, 28, 36, 104, 126
Muffins Made Simple 27
Mushrooms 21, 22, 31, 36, 37, 45, 74, 79, 85, 86, 99

N

Neopolitan-Style Pizza Dough 112
Never-Fail Buttercream 140
Nutritional Yeast 21, 22, 34, 35, 38, 39, 42, 44, 47, 55, 56, 62, 66, 67, 75, 77, 84, 85, 87, 94, 97, 145
Nuts
    Almond 20, 58, 94, 98, 119, 128, 135, 138, 139
    Cashews 35, 42, 48, 49, 63, 66, 75, 94, 99, 134
    Peanut 48, 80, 137
    Pecans 25, 68, 69, 90, 105, 122, 132, 133
    Pignolis 94, 135
    Pistachio 23, 124, 130
    Walnuts 23, 65, 67, 132, 134

O

Olives 41, 64, 67, 111
Olive Tapenade 41
Onions 34, 36, 37, 45, 46, 47, 49, 57, 58, 62, 68, 70, 72, 75, 77, 76, 85, 86, 88, 90, 91, 92, 95, 98, 99
Oranges 105, 118

P

Parsley Cashew Dipping Sauce 49
Pasta 44, 45, 47, 55, 56, 66, 75, 76, 80, 100, 101
Peanut Butter 48, 107, 137
Peanut Sauce 48
Pears 128, 129
Peas 45, 66
Pepper
    Bell 52, 66, 70, 91, 95, 96
Prosecco 29, 145
Prosecco Cherry Chia Jam 29
Piña Colada Upside-Down Cornmeal Cake 122
Pineapple 109, 122, 123, 130
Pizzelles 139
Poached Pears With Meringue and Chocolate Drizzle 128
Poolish 105, 110, 111, 145
Potato Cheese Pierogi 76

Potatoes
- Bliss 34
- Sweet 22, 67, 95
- Yam 95
- Yukon Gold 22, 32, 59, 77

Potato Radicchio Salad with Walnut/Kalamata Olive Pesto 67
Pumpkin 25, 47, 58, 133
Pumpkin Pecan Chocolate Magic Bars 133

R

Radicchio 67
Radishes 21
Ras El Hanout 42, 145
Raw Key Lime Bars 134
Real-Deal Light and Airy Doughnuts 106
Rice 37, 52, 54, 70, 72, 88, 89, 90, 94, 95, 119
- Rice Flour 28, 117, 119, 126, 131, 140
- Rice Paper 80
- Rice Syrup 55, 104, 137
- Rice Vinegar 48, 50, 64, 66

Roasted Brussels Sprouts, Apples, Cranberries and Walnut Salad 65
Roasted Celery, Leek and Potato Soup With Bacon and Gremolata Garnish ... 59
Roasted Red Pepper Chimichurri 48
Roasted Tomato & Grilled Corn Chutney Quinoa Salad 68

S

Saffron 42, 44, 47, 119, 145
Sambuca 119, 145
Scones 23
Seitan 59, 84, 113, 146
Shallots 36, 37, 48, 53, 54, 55, 65, 86
Shumai Dumplings 74
Simple Syrup 81, 118, 146
Smoky Kale and Potato Casserole 98
Sourdough 26, 100, 112, 146
Sourdough Pasta 100
Spanish Rice and Bean Salad 70
Spiced Pumpkin Seeds 58
Spicy Chili Sauce 91

Spiked Maple Butter 29
Spinach. 34, 64, 75, 84, 85, 113
Spinach Ricotta 75
Struffoli 138
Stuffed Mushrooms With An Herb Oil Drizzle 36
Sweet & Sour Dipping Sauce 49
Swiss Cheese 86, 87

T

Tahini 40, 80, 87, 131, 146
Tempeh 62, 95, 146
Thai Corn Coconut Soup 55
Tofu Scramble 21
Tomato 42, 45, 46, 47, 49, 52, 68, 69, 90, 91, 95, 111, 113
Tomato Gravy 46, 75, 84, 94, 100
Tomato Mango Lime Salsa 49
Tourlou - Greek Ratatouille. 92
Turmeric. 21, 35, 44, 55

V

Vegetable Cannelloni 75
Vermouth 86, 146
Vital Wheat Gluten 84, 146

W

Winter Rolls 80

Y

Yellow Squash 66

Z

Za'atar. 64, 146
Za'atar Seasoning 64
Zucchini 26, 66, 75
Zucchini Muffins 26

ACKNOWLEDGMENTS

This cookbook would have never been possible without the love, support and honest feedback from so many people. It has been a dream of mine since I was a young girl learning my way in the kitchen.

That being said, I suppose I'll start at the beginning to express my gratitude and appreciation to those whose influence in my life germinated the inspiration for this book.

Mary McCran, my maternal grandmother, recognized that experiential learning was how I best assimilated new knowledge into my being. Her loving kindness and patience as she walked me through her recipes, most of which were in her head, taught me how to not only cook and bake but possibly more importantly, how to trust my culinary instincts.

And, of course, there is the legendary Julia Child, whose "if I can do it, you can too" attitude was the encouragement I needed early on. Progress not perfection, perseverance to keep trying even when it didn't turn out quite as I had hoped, and the inquisitiveness to try unfamiliar ingredients are characteristics instilled in me from all the years of watching and reading anything and everything that Julia Child created.

ME ROCKIN' MY CUSTOM-MADE-FOR-ME KAT MENDENHALL BOOTS

To Myss Miranda, whose professionalism, graphic design prowess, and superior development nerdiness brought my dream of being a published cookbook author into reality. The book you are currently holding in your hands is a direct result of her ability to listen and understand my vision, coupled with her wickidly impressive eye for design.

PAINTED BY DAWSON NALDER

To all my students who participated in my Veganification® Boutique Culinary classes and to the attendees and friends of my Veganification® - Verde Valley Vegans Meetup potlucks and dinners, from those who were veg-curious to staunch vegans, thank you for being willing taste testers, providing me with honest feedback. The recipes contained in this cookbook were all possible because of your discerning palates. I would be remiss if I didn't give special shout-outs to Ann Decker, who stayed after every single class helping me clean up until the last piece of silverware was cleaned and put away; to Rose Campisi, who never left my sink until every area was spotless after every potluck; to Kris Greene, for her constant dedication to capturing the fun via photos; and to Annette McGregor, who has the uncanny ability to verbalize what her tastebuds sense, especially when there was a constructive criticism that pushed me to do better.

While I incessantly talked about writing this book for countless years, it wasn't until I attended Victoria Moran's Main Street Vegan Academy that I realized I had the courage to actually see it to fruition. In addition to Victoria, it was people like fellow alumni J.L. Fields, Kat Moss Mendenhall, and Naomi Green, who followed their passions to become a vegan culinary instructor and cookbook author, a purveyor of awesome vegan cowboy boots and other accessories (check out the photo of my custom-made-for-me boots which I like to think are a cross between a cowgirl boot and a 1960's go-go boot), and a vegan health coach and retreat guru, respectively, that brought me back to the "if I can do it, you can too" attitude.

To my three chosen sisters in life, Janet Hill, Liz Campbell and Susheel "Sue" Godara, your friendship, sisterhood, love, and support throughout the years have been pillars of strength.

To Dawson Nalder, whose artistic talent manifested my vision of having my logo background show up on my chef's jacket and sneakers, thank you! Outstanding! If you are interested in having Dawson create something wonderful and unique for you, he can be reached at @StormCustomDesigns on Instagram.

To my family, without whom none of this would ever have been possible. To my Dad, Ed Voorhis, to whom this book has been dedicated, my always-willing omnivore who thoroughly enjoyed eating anything I'd create. To my mother, Ida Voorhis, for teaching me how to be organized and disciplined. To my son, Jason Matano, for his constant ribbing. Your sense of humor and ability to embrace a mother who doesn't necessarily fit the mold of a traditional parent (to quote you, "snowflake"), I love you dearly and am so proud of your adventurous culinary spirit. To my Grandsons, Jason and Kristopher, the apples didn't fall far from the tree. Love you to infinity and beyond.

MY SON, JASON, WITH GRANDSONS, JASON AND KRISTOPHER

And no list of thanks would be complete if I didn't include the four-leggeds that rescued me throughout the years, from Pierre, Midnight, Samantha, Cleo, Pharoah, Gypsy, Tasha, and Maizie. My house would never feel quite like a home without you. Your companionship, your ability to know exactly when I need a hug, or a lick on my face, is astonishing and heartfelt.

To all of you who are veg-curious or are somewhere on the path to becoming vegan, thank you for each time you choose to eat a plant-based meal. And finally, to those of you who have already adopted a vegan lifestyle, thank you for embracing the practice of Ahimsa, being dedicated to causing the least harm and the most good -- for the animals, for the planet, for your own health and wellbeing.

ABOUT LINDA

Linda Voorhis is a vegan culinary instructor and founder of Veganification®, Veganification®/Verde Valley Vegans Facebook Group, and the Verde Valley Vegans Meetup.

Linda is a Main Street Vegan Academy Master Vegan Lifestyle Coach and Educator. She earned her Certificate for Plant-Based Nutrition from the Center for Nutrition Studies at Cornell University.

"A passionate cook since I was literally old enough to stir a spoon in a pot, becoming vegan has transformed my love for cooking and baking into the process that I refer to as "Veganification®." It includes developing original recipes and converting non-vegan recipes into sumptuous vegan versions that will knock the socks off any plant-based eater. Possibly even more important is being able to create offerings that omnivores are equally impressed with and delightfully devour.

For me, being vegan is a lifestyle, not just a food plan. It is the compassionate way that I step into my life on a daily basis as a human being and vegan activist. It is also important for my personal health and wellbeing, for all sentient beings, for the environment, and for the planet."

In The Spirit of Ahimsa,

Linda Voorhis

VISIT VEGANIFICATION.COM
to subscribe to Linda's blog and find out about upcoming events

YOU CAN FOLLOW LINDA @VEGANIFICATION

Do you have a question regarding a recipe, a procedure, or anything else in this book--such as, how could I convert a particular recipe to whole food, to no added oil, or to gluten-free, please go to **VEGANIFICATION.COM/ASKLINDA** and ask your question. I will personally respond to questions submitted through this link.

ABOUT VEGANIFICATION®

Veganification® celebrates the journey of becoming and being vegan. Our mission is to provide vegan holistic wellness and lifestyle activities that include education, advocacy, and activism. At the core is the promotion of self-actualization, building community, and environmental sustainability. We proudly host vegan culinary demonstrations and classes, personalized individual and group coaching, and speaking engagements. We also work closely with restaurants to help them develop vegan-friendly menus and organize Vegan Nights Out.

If you are interested in learning more about any of these activities, please email Info@Veganification.com

PHOTO CREDITS

TITLE	LICENSE	PHOTOGRAPHER	PAGE
Cover Photo	Linda Voorhis	Covers, iii, ix
Linda and her Dad	Linda Voorhis	vii
Linda in the Front Yard	Linda Voorhis	ix
My Ahimsa Tattoo - freshly finished	Linda Voorhis	xi
Green Vegetables on White	Motion Array	Chzu	x, xi
Abstract Art Cooking Cutlery	Pixabay	xii, xiii, xiii, xiv, xv
Chef JL Fields 2018	JL Fields	17
JL Fields 2018	JL Fields	17
Vegetables Collection	Envato Elements	Karandaev	18, 32, 60, 93, 102, 114
Muffins with Bananas	Envato Elements	Alexandraanschiz	19
Hashbrown Waffles	Linda Voorhis	22
Homemade Blueberry Breakfast Scones	Envato Elements	Bhofack2	23
Homemade Cornbread Muffins	Envato Elements	Bhofack2	24
Pecan Nuts	Envato Elements	Arzamasova	25
Zucchini Muffins	Linda Voorhis	26
Vegan Blueberry Muffins	Pixabay	27
Coconut Milk in The Glass Bottle	Envato Elements	Alinakho	28
Lemons	Envato Elements	Hit Delight	28
Lemon Citrus Fruit Juicy Juice	Pixabay	28
Cherries	Pixabay	29
Maple Syrup	Envato Elements	Dream79	29
Mushrooms. Fresh Mushrooms in Basket	Envato Elements	Sea Wave	30, 31, 36
Homemade Flakey Buttermilk Biscuits	Envato Elements	Bhofack2	31
Traditional Greek Sauce	Envato Elements	Yuliya Furman	33
Red Potatoes	Envato Elements	Bill Berry Photography	34
Olive Oil and Herbs	Envato Elements	Grafvision	36
Olives, Olive Oil and Ciabatta	Envato Elements	Nadianb	40
Olives	Envato Elements	Gresei	41, 67
Heap Of Cashew Nuts	Envato Elements	Picture Partners	42
Garlic	Envato Elements	Gresei	42
Various Sauces. Popular Sauces in Bowls	Envato Elements	Karandaev	43
Gravy Boat on Gray Slate Free Space	Envato Elements	Denis Karpenkov	44
Hollandaise Sauce	Envato Elements	Peter Hermes Furian	44
Ingredients For Spaghetti Bolognese	Envato Elements	Merinka	45
Autumn Leaves and Pumpkins	Envato Elements	Haveseen	47
Cutting Board At Black	Envato Elements	Seregam	51
Vegan Cream Soups	Envato Elements	Alexandraanschiz	51
Tomato Soup Gazpacho	Pixabay	52
Raw Haricot Legumes Cannellini Beans	Envato Elements	Duskbabe	53
Rice Grains Food Eat	Pixabay	54
Tai Corn Soup	Linda Voorhis	55
Bowl and Napkin	Envato Elements	Alex9500	55
Dry Macaroni Pasta	Envato Elements	Leungchopan	56
Fresh Cauliflower on Wooden Board	Envato Elements	Sea Wave	56
Homemade Organic Black Bean Soup	Envato Elements	Bhofack2	57

PHOTO CREDITS

Vibrant Green Fresh Leek Vegetable	Envato Elements | Merc67	59
Chopped Celery Sticks	Envato Elements | Pineapple Studio	59
Vegan Food Background	Envato Elements | Nadianb	61
Green Apples	Envato Elements | Bogdandreava	62
Romaine Lettuce	Envato Elements | Alex_Star	63
Romaine Lettuce	Envato Elements | Cynoclub	63
Dill with Twine on Granite Table	Envato Elements | Rezkrr	63
Roasted Brussels Sprouts on A Foil	Envato Elements | Edalin	65
Peeled Walnuts	Envato Elements | Picture Partners	67
Whole Single Fresh Radicchio	Envato Elements | Picture Partners	67
Roasted Cherry Tomatoes with Herbs	Envato Elements | Annapustynnikova	68
Uncooked Quinoa	Envato Elements | Oxana Denezhkina	68
Grilled Corn, Food Border Background	Envato Elements | Merc67	69
Black Beans Rice with Cilantro	Envato Elements | Arzamasova	70
Tortilla	Envato Elements | Mythja	71
Dolma. Stuffed Grape Leaves with Rice	Envato Elements | Tim Olina	72, 73
Potato Cheese Pierogis	Envato Elements | Daniel Dash	77
Sushi Black Slate and Chopsticks	Envato Elements | Hit Delight	78
Egg Roll Spring Roll	Envato Elements | Kbmars	79
Tamales	Pixabay	81
Creme Anglaise	Wikimedia Commons | David Monniaux	82
Healthy Vegan Food Concept	Freepik	83
King Oyster Mushroom 1	Envato Elements | Gita Kulinica	87
King Oyster Mushroom 2	Envato Elements | Gita Kulinica	87
Homemade Black Bean Soup	Envato Elements | Iuliia N	88
Mango Sticky Rice	Linda Voorhis	89
A Small Pile Of Chopped Red Onions	Envato Elements | Gcpics	90
Organic Pecan	Envato Elements | K Jekol	90, 91
Fresh Green Jalapeno Peppers and Slices	Envato Elements | Picture Partners	90, 91
Brown Unrefined Cane Sugar	Envato Elements | Katrinshine	91
Raw Lentils in a Metallic Scoop	Envato Elements | Rawf8	91
Hot Tomato Sauce	Envato Elements | Vikif	91
Greek Tourlou	Linda Voorhis	92
Heart of Palm on Cutting Board	Myss Miranda	93
Fresh Organic Red Bell Pepper	Envato Elements | Bhofack2	96, 97
Bunch Of Freshly Harvested Carrots	Envato Elements | Lana M	96, 97
Fresh Green Cauliflower	Envato Elements | Picture Partners	96, 97
Fresh Yellow Cauliflower	Envato Elements | Picture Partners	96, 97
Leek	Envato Elements | Ivankmit	97
Closeup of Fresh Butternut Squash	Envato Elements | Rawpixel	97
Kale	Envato Elements | Arzamasova	98
Potatoes Yellow with Parsley	Envato Elements | Rezkrr	98
Bucatini	Linda Voorhis	101
Rigatoni Pile	Linda Voorhis	101
Delicious Fresh Bread	Envato Elements | Tommyandone	103
Muffins	Linda Voorhis	104
Muffins in Pan	Linda Voorhis	104
Cherry Orange Pecan Country Loaf	Linda Voorhis	105
Morning Breakfast with Mini Donuts	Envato Elements | Merinka	106

Homemade Donuts with Sugar	Envato Elements | Merinka	107
White Marble Natural Texture Background	Envato Elements | Formatoriginal	108, 109
Homemade White Wheat Bread	Envato Elements | Natasha Breen	108, 109
Sourdough for Baking Bread	Envato Elements | Natasha Breen	108, 109
Homemade Italian Focaccia Flatbread	Envato Elements | Sonya Kamoz	110
Fresh Raw Dough	Envato Elements | Magone	112
Calzone Stuffed with Kite Hill Ricotta	Linda Voorhis	113
White Plaster Wall Closeup	Envato Elements | Vvoennyy	115
Chocolate Stout Cake	Linda Voorhis	115, 121
Limoncello Coconut Cake	Linda Voorhis	117
Homemade Limoncello	Envato Elements | Motghnit	118
Italian Saffron Rice Torta	Linda Voorhis	119
Pina Colada Upside Cake	Linda Voorhis	123
Dried Date Fruit in Wooden Bowl	Envato Elements | J Chizhe	124
Pistachio Nuts	Envato Elements | Kjekol	124
Pistachio Nuts on Wooden Background	Envato Elements | Sea Wave	125
Pizzelles	Unsplash | Isabella And Louisa Fischer	127, 139
Chocolate Fondant Preparation	Envato Elements | Denis Karpenkov	128
Fruit Fresh Pears	Pixabay	129
Lemon Chocolate Sweet and Sour	Pixabay	129
Nixon, Republican National Convention	Getty Images | Rolls Press	130
Pistachio Bowl	Envato Elements | Bill Berry Photography	130
Pineapple on Yellow	Envato Elements | Valeria Aksakova	130
Marshmallow	Envato Elements | Tycoon101	131
Sliced and Whole Blood Oranges	Envato Elements | Nblxer	131
Half Blood Orange	Envato Elements | Grafvision	131
Sweet Cake with Cut Strawberry	Envato Elements | Jultud	131
Sweet Cake with Chocolate Threads	Envato Elements | Jultud	131
Chockate Sauce	Envato Elements | Tycoon101	132
Limes	Pixabay	134
Grandma Mary's Pignoli Cookies	Linda Voorhis	135
Coconut Chocolate-Dipped Cookies	Linda Voorhis	136
Homemade Sweet Italian Struffoli	Envato Elements | Bhofack2	138
Homemade Cupcake with Buttercream	Envato Elements | Natasha Breen	140
Green Smoothie in Glass Jar	Envato Elements | J Chizhe	141, 142, 143
Linda in Kat Mendenhall Boots	Linda Voorhis	155
Sneakers by Dawson Nalder	Linda Voorhis	156
Jason & Grandsons	Linda Voorhis	157
Linda in the Lemongrass	Linda Voorhis	158

www.ingramcontent.com/pod-product-compliance
Lightning Source LLC
Chambersburg PA
CBHW061753290426
44108CB00029B/2983